W9-BXG-851

Seeds of Hope

Blessings,
Terese Holloway
Ps. 46:10

Seeds of Hope

TERESE HOLLOWAY

CREATION
HOUSE
A STRANG COMPANY

SEEDS OF HOPE by Terese Holloway
Published by Creation House
A Strang Company
600 Rinehart Road
Lake Mary, Florida 32746
www.strangbookgroup.com

All Scripture quotations are from the New King James Version of the Bible. Copyright © 1979, 1980, 1982 by Thomas Nelson, Inc., publishers. Used by permission.

Design Director: Bill Johnson
Cover design by Justin Evans

Author photo courtesy of Special Moments, Lubbock, Texas.

Library of Congress Control Number: 2010920440
International Standard Book Number: 978-1-61638-146-2

First Edition

10 11 12 13 14 — 9 8 7 6 5 4 3 2 1
Printed in the United States of America

DEDICATION

I WOULD LIKE TO DEDICATE *Seeds of Hope* to my sweet cousin Debbie DelaRosa and my dear friends Jacque McIver and her husband, Glen. Debbie, Jacque, and Glen have all inspired me to trust in the Lord, even in the midst of difficult times. Debbie, who has suffered through months in a cancer treatment center for multiple myeloma, has taught me the importance of not giving up but believing God can do *all* things, even when it seems impossible!

Jacque and Glen lost their only son, Bradford, nineteen years old, to a tragic death. They have endured what no parent should ever have to go through! I cannot imagine the heartache and grief which is beyond words, but through it all, they have remained an inspiration to many!

Both of these families have inspired me to write *Seeds of Hope* so that others can also find comfort and peace in difficult times! I bless both of these families in my life and pray the Lord will continue to minister healing, comfort, and hope in the midst of their lives.

> Blessed be the God and Father of our Lord Jesus Christ, the Father of mercies and God of all comfort, who comforts us in all our tribulation, that we may be able to comfort those who are in any trouble, with the comfort with which we ourselves are comforted by God. For as the sufferings of Christ abound in us, so our consolation also abounds through Christ.
>
> —2 CORINTHIANS 1:3–5

INTRODUCTION

NUMEROUS CHRISTIANS DEAL ON a daily basis with those things structured, by the enemy, to steal their peace, joy, and well being. Sometimes a word of encouragement is all they need to reaffirm to them, in their times of distress, that God is still there and their cries do not go unheard. Even in difficult times, God is always faithful to plant seeds of love and encouragement to those with ears to hear.

Seeds of Hope is a book to encourage and lift up those who feel downtrodden.

The Father's heart is to change lives and cause destinies to be reached. His desire is to reward those who stand by faith in difficult times. The Father's heart is to change lives. He is looking for those who will trust Him to see them through, no matter what the circumstances may portray. He enriches lives through the power of His blood, working always to accomplish great and mighty things, beyond what could be imagined.

This book was birthed to help sustain those who have become weary and tired in well doing; to open the eyes of those who are seeking the Lord for answers even when there seems to be no way out. This book is for the one who desires to walk in the kingdom of God and trust God for the impossible, believing that He is more than able to do exceedingly and abundantly, above all that we could ever ask or think.

God wants to encourage the broken, the tired, the weary, and the faithful with reassurance that He is always there. He will never leave nor forsake! His heart is to lead His children into their destiny and to raise them to higher heights than they have ever gone before. By faith, He is calling the hearts of His children to trust Him for the answers even when they cannot see. He offers seeds of hope to help those in need as they continue to climb the mountains set before them.

He leads, He guides, He comforts, and He soothes. He gives hope to the hopeless, light in the darkness, and restoration to those who are seeking His answers. He merely breathes, and miracles are thrust into motion. Faith grows and lives change when God's children cry out to Him.

May you be encouraged to seek God, one day at a time, as seeds of hope are planted in your heart. Trust the Holy Spirit to water the seeds and bring to fruition God's perfect plan for your life!

The Breath of Dawn
Most High and Secret Place
Endurance Brings Gain
Deliverance from the Fowler's Deadly Snare
He's in Control
Lifting the Burdens
Creator of All
Many Are Your Wonders
Blessings Follow Pain
Bathed in Love
Growing in Grace
His Light in Me
Joy of the Morning
Spirit of Truth
Designed by His Hand
Sunshine of His Presence
The Light That Leads
Portrait of Grace
Anointing Oil from Heaven
Courage of His Presence
The Sparrow in the Storm
Called to Bear a Burden
Mighty in Battle Are the Saints of the Lord
Only You
Marked for Success
Wondrous Works
Your Victory Is a Stone's Throw Away
Window of God
Restoration of Love
Set Your Hope Upon God
Until He Comes to Call Me Home

JANUARY

THE BREATH OF DAWN

All creation stood in silence, as the winds began to blow;
The Breath of Dawn kissed heaven, from earth's valley far below.
The sky began to shimmer, inside the morning light;
Darkness bowed to solace—and vanished with the night.
Tiny dewdrops sparkled, upon the landscape's lawn;
And fragrance rode the gentle breeze, upon the Breath of Dawn.
The birds began a melody, that touched the heart of God;
And hope became the PROMISE, that lifted up in song.
A new day in creation, unfolds before our eyes;
Our hearts are lifted upward, and we're called to greater heights.
He breathes His breath upon us—our dependence is on God;
He opens heaven's doorway, and gives us wings to ride the dawn!

JANUARY 2

MOST HIGH AND SECRET PLACE

Lord, may I never wander, into any realm unknown;
Instead, I'll set my compass, toward the footstool of Your throne.
And when I come across a trial that causes me to shake;
May You use it in my life—to grow me in my faith.
I pray my worries will not rob me, of what tomorrow plans to
  bring;
Nor sorrow steal away from me, the songs I've yet to sing.
And when I find myself alone, in places that I dread;
Lord, open heaven's portal and be the lifter of my head.
I pray You'll help me focus and not surrender to my fears;
That You'll draw me to Your bosom and wipe away my tears.
Lord, let my wild imagination no longer have its way
Nor let it paint a doomsday picture that will draw my heart
  astray.
Instead, Lord, help me dwell, within YOUR Secret Place Most
  High
Inside Your realm of Glory—where I've been given wings to fly.
Take me, Lord, BEHIND the veil, where true love speaks release;
Where Your breath of sweet anointing—breathes the fragrance of
  Your peace.
Yes, Lord, cause my heart to seek You and Your all-consuming
  grace;
Within YOUR Walls of Glory—in Your Most High AND Secret
  Place!

ENDURANCE BRINGS GAIN

The weight of life's burdens are often heavy to bear;
And the strength to arise is not always there.
You see, God never promised a life without pain;
But He assured our endurance, would always bring gain.
So, even though weary and pierced with despair;
Look up, into Glory, and you'll see Him there.
For, He will not lead you, where He would not go;
Instead, He'll be there, in life's highs AND lows.
Yes, He will give strength, to go the next mile
To overcome struggles and face every trial
And for those who endure and overcome through it all;
Will gain rich rewards and be closer to God.
For, it's the hands of the sculptor that refine us as gold;
It's HIS holy fire that sets us aglow.
So, the next time life's trials, bring you great pain;
Remember, HIS Promise—and Let Endurance Bring Gain!

JANUARY 4

DELIVERANCE FROM THE FOWLER'S DEADLY SNARE

Deliver me, Oh, Lord, from the fowler's deadly snare;
And hide me in Your shelter—safe within Your care
With mighty hands extended, rescue me from harm
Reach out and pull me in, to the safety of Your arms.
Defend my territory and release Your justice, Lord;
Against defiant foes with their ever-ready swords.
Bring victory out of chaos, turn my darkness into light;
Breathe Your breath upon me and set my wings to flight.
Open heaven's portal and cause my eyes to see;
The wonder of Your Kingdom and all You've done for me.
Lord, provide a sanctuary where I can come to You
When I'm feeling overpowered and constantly pursued.
Deliver me, Oh, Lord, from the fowler's deadly snare
Chase my foes away and let me rest within Your care.

JANUARY 5

HE'S IN CONTROL

Life is so very fragile, and without warning it can change;
We never are for certain, that every day will stay the same.
We may not always understand, God's plan from day to day;
Nor the detours we will find, as we walk along life's way.
But one thing is for certain, God's in control and always near;
To comfort and console, bring peace and calm each fear.
And we know that every evil, God will surely turn around;
We'll find that when we seek Him, there's no doubt, He will be
found.
So, with grateful hearts we praise Him for the miracles displayed;
On behalf of every saint that bowed a burdened heart to pray.
As we recognize His presence and see His mighty plan unfold;
May it help us see more clearly, and understand—He's in Control.

Lifting the Burdens

When the weight of my burdens, are too much to bear;
I send them to Jesus, on the wings of a prayer.
My burdens are lifted and placed upon Him;
They are no longer mine—they have NOW become His!
Then I must leave every burden, in His faithful hands;
And trust Him, in battle, until it all finally ends!
It's not always easy, and I'm not always quick;
To lift up to Jesus, what is making me SICK!
But, He, holds the answers, and He holds the key;
To the weight of my burdens, and deliverance for me.
So, I will exchange, every burden and care;
By lifting them up—on the wings of a prayer!
I will take on HIS yoke, for it's easy and light;
I will no longer struggle, because, NOW, it's HIS fight!
In the midst of it all, I'll place my burdens on HIM;
They are no longer mine—NOW, they are HIS!

JANUARY 7

CREATOR OF ALL

Who brings forth LIFE, in the form of a seed;
And creates a small heart, THEN commands it to BEAT?
Who walks the sand on the ocean's vast shore;
And stretches His hand to the depths of its floor?
Who thrusts the stardust across the black sky;
And paints heaven's masterpiece, night after night?
Who holds the world in the palm of His hand;
And blows His sweet breath, to cover its land?
Who made the grass and the valleys so low;
And the majestic white mountains, covered in snow?
Who gave us EVERYTHING, we'd ever need;
The sun and the stars, and the air that we breathe?
Who, in His Glory, would love us SO MUCH;
To give His OWN Son, to die for US?
Who, but the Father, would sacrifice ALL;
In order to save, and restore man's great fall?
Who, in His Love, gave provision and grace;
To draw and extend, His arms of embrace?
Oh, that we'd SEE, His exquisite display;
And give Him, our lives, and our hearts filled with Praise.
For, He is the artist—the Almighty God;
He's the Alpha, Omega—CREATOR OF ALL.

MANY ARE YOUR WONDERS

Lord, You've made all things beautiful, and put Your love inside of
   men—
God, my heart can't even fathom, Your beginning OR Your end!
I cannot probe Your limits or the mysteries of Your Grace;
For they are higher than the heavens and reach beyond the
   deepest grave.
Lord, Your thoughts are not my thoughts, nor are Your ways my
   ways within;
For Your thoughts and ways are higher, than what MY mind
   could comprehend.
Yes, You, Oh Lord, are seated and exalted upon the throne;
Where angels cry out, "Holy," and heaven is Your home.
It was You who formed the mountains, and created blowing
   winds;
It was You who colored sunsets and revealed Your heart to men.
Yes, MANY Are Your Wonders, Lord—and great are ALL Your
   works;
And I know that You're enthroned above, the heavens and the
   earth.
So, I lift my eyes unto the skies, past the beauty of the stars;
To see You as Creator, AND acknowledge WHO You are!
Yes, You, Oh Sovereign God, have given EVERYTHING its birth;
Oh Lord, You've manifested greatness, through your awesome
   handiwork!
So, when I look around me and witness all that YOU have made;
I will honor You FOREVER and NEVER cease to give You praise!

JANUARY 9

BLESSINGS FOLLOW PAIN

To deny myself and follow Christ, means I must get rid of—ME;
For I can only follow Him, if I'm where, I'M supposed to be.
You see, when I get myself together, everything may seem to
    change;
But, I'll ONE day see the blessings—on the OTHER side of pain!
Because, it's only in the process, and where I'm called to walk;
That will lead me into greatness—into the PRESENCE of my
    God.
So, today, my scars remind me of ALL that has been done;
So that I can walk in victory, until this war, is finally won.
I know it's, IN, the turmoil, and all that stirs within;
That causes me to rise above—and Truly, Follow Him!

BATHED IN LOVE

Alive and well forever,
Lost completely in His Word;
Basking in the sunshine,
Of the treasure of God's worth!
Soaking in His presence,
Bathed Within His Love,
Covered by His mercy,
Receiving blessings from above!

JANUARY 11

GROWING IN GRACE

(Read Luke 12:27)

Consider the lily with beauty so rare;
Nurtured by God and His infinite care.
Arrayed in His splendor, clothed from above;
Touched by His Grace, and growing in love.
If God in His Glory, can clothe the earth's field;
What more can He do, for those seeking His Will?
He'll watch over the heart and each seed planted there,
With His most gentle touch, and His own tender care.
And just like the lily, with its beauty unique;
That covers the landscape, and makes it complete—
We, too, are the special work of His hands;
Each one created, as a part of His plan.
And no matter WHERE, He leads us by faith;
We are constantly learning and Growing in Grace!

HIS LIGHT IN ME

I look out into the darkness, across the stormy skies
I can hardly take it in nor scarce believe my eyes.
For the waves are crashing high and the winds in tempest blow;
Lightening flashes in succession, with such devastating bolts.
But I am safe within the storm, for I'm a lighthouse straight and
tall;
I do not swerve or swagger, nor do I fear I'll fall.
Instead my light is powerful, as it pierces through the night
Giving hope to weary travelers, and a point to fix their sight.
Yes, the winds may come and fiercely blow—the waves may rock
the shore;
But THIS lighthouse will be steady, even in the raging storm.
For I am anchored in foundation, to the one true living light;
And because He lives within me—THIS lighthouse will burn
bright.
I will always be found sturdy when the storms of life appear;
Even in the darkest hour, I promise I'll be here.
So, if you should find yourself, inside the crashing waves
With darkness all around you, lost within its thunderous rage
Will you look up to Jesus, until you see His light in me;
And then trust Him to deliver you, from the raging sea?
You see, the light of Christ burns in me, to direct you to HIS
shore;
To the place where you'll find solace, in the presence of the Lord.
For it's the Father's love that pierces, through the darkest night;
I am just a vessel—a house that holds His light.
But I will always be there, standing steady in the storm
To point you toward Jesus and help you make it to the shore.
You see, He has placed me as a lighthouse, upon the raging sea
Yes, He filled me with His Spirit and He put HIS Light in Me!

JANUARY 13

JOY OF THE MORNING

Morning breaks upon the dawn, as darkness yields to light;
And praise explodes upon creation, calling everything to life.
The tiny sparrows find their voices, and offer up their song;
For the night has given way, to the early morning dawn.
Like lovely gems, the dew drops sparkle, with exquisite beauty to
  behold;
Seems its seed that has been scattered, of brilliant jewels and
  shiny gold.
Simply splashed across the canvas, a brand new masterpiece each
  day;
It's the portrait of God's Love—and the goodness of His Grace!
It's the Lord's most awesome promise, that darkness always yields
  to light;
And that the Joy of the Morning, will always wash away the night!

January 14

Spirit of Truth

In the midst of our lives, God is moving HIS way;
He's breathing NEW life, and He's sending HIS rain.
Exploding with power, God's Spirit's alive;
Bearing wonderful fruit, and a passion divine.
The Spirit of Truth, and HIS wonders revealed;
Come from hunger and thirst, and a desire to be filled.
Living water from God, poured out from above;
Transformed in His presence, engulfed in His love.
Addicted with passion, and Spirit-filled lives;
With hearts that are yearning and yielded to Christ!

JANUARY 15

DESIGNED BY HIS HAND

In such a short time, you've already sustained;
The heartache of loss, and deep suffering pain.
But the Lord, never once, took His eyes off of you;
He's been there all the time, always leading you through.
He saw you before, your life took its shape;
He charted your course, and the path you would take.
He precedes and He follows—He knows EVERYTHING;
He's always aware, of what tomorrow will bring!
You can NEVER be lost, or away from God's Love;
For He guides with His hand, and He leads from above!
Yes, you were created, for His own special plan;
Fashioned with love—and Designed by His Hand!

SUNSHINE OF HIS PRESENCE

The sunshine of God's presence, shines down to lead my way;
It lights the path before me, as I walk with Him each day.
He helps me see HIS vision, so I won't stumble, trip or fall;
He knows that I am fragile, so He helps me to stand tall.
He illuminates the darkness, and makes my victory sure;
He teaches me to walk upright, so my heart will be found pure.
The Sunshine of His Presence, is ALWAYS there to light my way;
To shine upon the road I walk—As I travel day to day!

JANUARY 17

THE LIGHT THAT LEADS

Sometimes life is a struggle, and so often makes no sense;
But my heart's secure in knowing, that God is my defense.
He ALWAYS gives me HOPE, in the midst of WHERE I am;
When I cannot figure out, what my mind can't understand.
So, TODAY, I'll see my problems, through the Father's loving
    eyes;
I will trust Him in the process and I will NOT compromise.
You see, God WILL Make the Difference, when I give my all to
    Him;
When I'm walking in HIS will, even when the light seems dim.
He will ALWAYS fight for me, so that I can hold my peace;
He is the path before me—He Is the Light That Leads!

January 18

Portrait of Grace

May those I come in contact with, be encouraged in their soul;
With eyes to see YOUR beauty and the love that Your heart
   holds.
May the gift of life that's in me, bring a glimpse of You today;
Through the witness of Your Glory and ALL that it portrays.
Yes, overwhelm me with Your beauty, let Your presence shine
   through me;
Draw others by Your Spirit—touch their hearts and set them free.
Lord, even in my darkest hour, and deepest trials, I will face;
Let the Beauty of Your Presence, reflect a Portrait of Your Grace!

JANUARY 19

ANOINTING OIL FROM HEAVEN

Lord, I pray You will equip me,
With strength to live for You;
And so I humbly yield my heart,
As a vessel for YOUR use!
Release a bold and holy passion—
Show me great and mighty things;
Lord, I even ask You, for the nations—
The hearts of Presidents and Kings!
Lift my sight to see You
In this place I'm called to be;
Touch my eyes with heaven's salve,
Perform Your perfect will in me.
Connect me to the olive tree,
And fill me 'til I'm full;
Then light the wick within me,
And let it burn Your holy fuel.
Set my heart aflame with fire,
Until it is totally ablaze;
Release me for Your Kingdom—
And lead me all my days!
Yes, pour out YOUR anointing oil
And Fill my heart 'til it's consumed;
May You cause my cup to overflow—
Everyday with MORE of YOU!

COURAGE OF HIS PRESENCE

When the storm is all around you, and you feel trapped inside the
 boat;
Line your mind up with your spirit—trust the Lord, and DON'T
 lose hope!
Speak to the raging waters, and the blowing of the winds;
Look inside the depth of fear, and let God put HIS peace within!
For, only God can calm the storm and remove its thunderous
 roar;
By calling you to rise above, and trust HIM in the storm.
You see, the Lord, will never take you to a place He will not be;
Whether in the lush green meadow or the harsh and blowing sea!
He's well aware of where you are, His eyes are locked on you;
And by His love, His grace abounds, and He will see you through!
So, when the storm surrounds you and you're tossed by blowing
 winds;
Remember, Christ is with you, He's alive and well within!
Take your authority in Jesus—Stand up Inside the Boat;
And let the Courage of His Presence, be the lifeline of your hope!

JANUARY 21

THE SPARROW IN THE STORM

From a tiny branch so small, the sparrow took to flight;
He spread his newly feathered wings and rose to greater heights.
Upon the thermal of the air, he soared upon the breeze;
Each time was higher than before, until he topped the tallest
    trees.
And then he heard the thunder roll and the wind began to blow;
His tiny wings grew weary, as he tried to hold his own.
But the storm grew fierce and brutal and he couldn't help but fall;
He lay broken, beat and wounded, beneath the weight of each
    raindrop.
The harshness of the season, seemed to bring a cruel end;
To the little sparrow's life, and his dreams of flight within.
But when the storm was over and the sun began to shine;
The sparrow found the strength, to stretch out his wings and fly.
He perched himself upon a branch and once again took flight;
He spread out his tiny wings, and flew away to greater heights.
You see, even little sparrows, learn to truly soar;
When the winds have finally ceased and they've made it through
    the storm.
So, if the Father watches sparrows, and is concerned to see them
    fly;
How much more is He persuaded, to care for you and I?
He will help us when we're weary—He'll keep us safe inside the
    storm;
He will give us wings like eagles and, Yes, He'll surely teach us—
    How to Soar!

CALLED TO BEAR A BURDEN

Called to Bear a Burden, she fell upon her knees;
Feeling hopelessly alone, completely robbed of inner peace.
She dared not to imagine, this heartache to its depth;
For fear, she would stop breathing and take her final breath.
The intensity of pain rumbled deep within her soul;
It grabbed her like a vice, with no plan of letting go.
Oh, how she longed for Jesus and HIS peace within her pain;
So, she bowed her heart to heaven and she called upon His
 Name.
She received His reassurance, that she would make it through;
But, she'd been Called to Bear a Burden, and intercede for YOU!
For a moment, God removed, what He knew YOU could not
 bear;
And He placed it on another, who would lift you up in prayer.
It's just His way of showing, His depth of love for you;
In the midst of inner turmoil and this place He's called you to.
Yes, He lifts your heavy load, dispersing evenly its weight;
He carries you on others' wings, and helps you in life's race.
So, when you FEEL forsaken, remember—God's STILL there;
And He's calling burden-bearers, to intercede for YOU—in
 prayer!

MIGHTY IN BATTLE ARE THE SAINTS OF THE LORD

In the valley of vision, I saw the Lord;
Like the Lion of Judah—He paced and He roared!
The time had come nigh for His warriors to move;
Prepared now and ready, to win and not lose.
Before Him, HIS Army, stood gathered for war;
Positioned for battle, that they might go forth.
They're sent out to conquer the enemy's plans;
They will NOT collapse, 'neath the strength of his hands.
For they are the predators, they're NOT the prey;
They have overcome death, even hell AND the grave.
They've the Keys of the Kingdom, possessing power in stride;
They WILL overcome evil, with the Lord on their side.
They walk in the Spirit—they submit to His Will;
They are clothed for the battle, in God's armor of steel.
Their position is righteous, yes, they are weapons of war;
They are Mighty in Battle—they're the Saints of the Lord!

ONLY YOU

Only You, Lord, hold the answers—only You, Lord, hold the keys;
To the questions in my heart, and my search for inner peace.
Only You, can give REAL meaning, to this life I daily live;
Only You, can give me comfort, and revive me once again.
Only You, can quench the thirst, when I feel as if I'll die;
When I've nothing left to offer, in my bruised and shattered life.
It's only by YOUR love, that I will truly be set free;
For Only You, Lord, hold the answers—
Only You, Lord, hold the keys!

JANUARY 25

MARKED FOR SUCCESS

When my focus is on You, Lord
Seems every THING just falls in place;
It's as if my steps are ordered
And my feet just walk in grace.
It's only when I put You first
That I will clearly see;
Your loving outstretched hand at work—
In ALL regarding me.
My brain can't even comprehend
All Your awesome blessings, Lord;
On this pathway stretched before me—
That leads to heaven's shore.
So, I'll embark upon this journey
With eyes securely fixed on You;
I will trust You, Lord, to open
Every door that I'll walk through.
I know in YOU there are no limits
In Your plans concerning me;
Your boundaries far exceed
What MY finite eyes can see.
For Your desire is to bless me
Beyond my wildest dreams;
So You Have Marked Me for Success,
To Accomplish Great and Mighty Things!

WONDROUS WORKS

From my inner depth of gratitude, my heart gives praise to You;
For all the Wondrous Works You've done, and all You've yet to
    do.
Yes, my eyes behold Your Glory, Lord, and Your magnificent
    display;
As the heavens and the earth applaud and creation shouts Your
    praise.
Humbly in Your presence, Lord, I know that everything must
    yield;
Giving way, to splendor—in accordance with Your Will.
For You, Oh Lord, are awesome—Your Spirit's in this place;
My eyes behold Your Glory and my heart is washed in Grace.
So, from my inner depth, Oh Lord, I give my praise to You;
For all the Wondrous Works You've done
And all You've yet to do!

JANUARY 27

YOUR VICTORY IS A STONE'S THROW AWAY

Put a guard upon your heart so that fear can't enter in;
Remember where you're headed and remember where you've
    been.
For it's truly in the battle, God WILL increase your strength;
To overcome victoriously, and keep you strong upon your feet.
You see, David killed Goliath, but FIRST a lion and a bear;
God never sent him to the giant, until he truly was prepared.
David stood and faced the battle, his faith in God was strong;
Yes, David threw the stone, but GOD guided it along.
So, even in the battle, when you face the devil's glare
Remember, God will never lead you, where you are unprepared.
So, stand up with mighty valor, upon your battlefield;
Trust God to fight for you, let him be your strength and shield.
For there is NO power greater, you will ever come to know;
Than trusting God by faith, knowing you are not alone.
So, rid your heart of fear and do not be afraid;
For your victory is so close—it's just a Stone's Throw Away!

WINDOW OF GOD

Only God's Window, in time can bring;
The bud of a rose, as it blooms in the spring!
Only the eyes, of the heart can behold;
The grace of HIS love, and ALL that it holds.
For each sun must set, and each flower die;
Here for a MOMENT, then lost from the eye!
It's God's open window, I peer through each day;
That allows me to see, His Love on Display!
His Riches Are Many—His Glory Divine
His Beauty Is Awesome, and His Blessings Are Mine!

RESTORATION OF LOVE

Only God can heal the broken heart,
Restore and make it new;
Only, He, knows just how DEEP the hurt,
And ALL you're going through!
He will blow away the winds,
And trials that cause you pain;
He will wipe away the tears
And remove their every stain.
He will breathe upon the emptiness
With a tender breath that soothes;
He will draw you by His Spirit,
And gently comfort you!
He will open heaven's porthole
And bid you, child, to come;
Into a place of refuge—
Lost, Inside His Love!

Set Your Hope Upon God

Set Your Hope Upon God, and His loving grace;
Be captured by Him, within His sweet embrace.
Receive HIS unmerited favor, through His very nature expressed;
Be loved by the Father—transformed, changed and blessed.
Now, YOU, are different, you're separated from sin;
You've been designed for a purpose, and dedicated to HIM!
So, don't fear the world's fears, nor hold dread in your heart;
Instead, sanctify ALL—for you're set apart.
Remember—God's in control, and HE reigns supreme;
He is MORE than enough, to conquer ALL things.
So adjust every attitude, and set your heart upon Him;
Be ready in season, to be peculiar, my friend.
You see, the Lord God IS Holy, and you're a picture of HIM;
You must understand DAILY, that you're predestined to win!
So, place your eyes upon Jesus, keep them focused and locked;
Trust COMPLETELY in Him—and Set Your Hope Upon God!

JANUARY 31

UNTIL HE COMES TO CALL ME HOME

I cannot peer into the future, without the eyes of God;
I know not what tomorrow brings, if I'll have life or not.
All I know is that TODAY, my life is in His hands;
So, I will do my best, to live according to HIS plan.
For in Him, my days are numbered, as I walk on earthly sod;
Because my life's lived in accordance with the calendar of God.
And when my life is over, He will carry me away;
Upon the wings of angels, where His light will never fade.
It's in His plan that I will live and follow where He leads;
Complete in self-assurance that He's forever watching me
So, even though I do not know, if I'll take another breath or not;
I'll put my trust upon this earth, into the loving hands of God.
And in His hands my heart will hold, the peace from Him alone;
To live my life with purpose—Until He Comes to Call Me Home!

Nothing Just Happens
Fisherman of Men
Our Destiny's Part of Your Plan
Sweet Oasis
Beginning and End
Heart Ablaze
His Light upon the Sunrise
Hope in the Midst of Transition
Captured for the Kingdom
Rest for My Soul
Behind the Veil
To Touch the Master's Garment
Shores of Heaven I'll Trod
His Anchor Always Holds
Miracles Still Happen
We Must Put Our Trust in Jesus
for the Victory Is the Lord's
How Many Times Will the Father Be There?
His Goodness, Love, and Mercy
The Potter's Wheel
Focused on Jesus
The Devil Takes a Fall
Somewhere in the Journey
God's Will Prevails
His Promise of the Spring
Imprints on the Seashore
Tears Are Simply Enough
Hinds Feet for High Places
Spring Will Prevail
Walking in the Ways of the Kingdom

FEBRUARY

FEBRUARY 1

NOTHING JUST HAPPENS

When I think about my life, and its every circumstance;
I'm reminded there is NOTHING—that happens just by chance.
I find I'm blessed in famine and also when I'm full;
You see, when Jesus deals with ME, He uses MANY different
    tools.
Yes, EVERYTHING has purpose, even death and pain;
Even when it makes no sense, God's working ALL things to my
    gain.
So, I will not turn my back on Him—for my God is NOT asleep;
My life is in HIS hands, and my walk, He'll surely keep.
You see, my steps have all been ordered, and my destiny is HIS;
He holds my heart securely, and He watches over it.
So, when I think about my life and its every circumstance;
I'm reminded there is NOTHING—that happens just by chance!

February 2

Fisherman of Men

I've traveled far past, hope's horizon, where depression's ruled my
  soul;
I've been immersed inside the darkness and lost within its hold.
And oftentimes, I've wondered if the Lord was really there;
If He could see my aching heart, or truly, IF He even cared.
Could He truly feel the pain, that held me in this vice;
Did He understand the depth, of this battle that I fight?
And then quickly, I was reminded of His overwhelming grace;
That swallows up the darkness and draws me IN, to His embrace.
I have felt Him touch my hand and pull me from death's very
  door;
Into His realm of glory, upon His throne room floor.
With a passion in my soul to move beyond all earthly hold;
Into HIS sanctuary—to the foot of heaven's throne.
A place where angels worship, where saints of God bow down;
Where the peace and love of Jesus, is all that can be found.
And in the midst of heaven's glory, God's Spirit spoke within;
He called upon my heart to be a fisherman of men.
For there are those around me who walk in darkness still;
Held captive by the enemy and bound to do his will.
They need to know the Savior and the grace that He bestows;
The love and peace of Jesus that freely flows from heaven's
  throne.
They need to see the light and be delivered from despair;
To know they're NOT alone—to KNOW that Jesus cares.
So, today, I'll trust in Jesus, to be a light in me;
To pierce the devil's darkness and set the captives free.
I will go where Jesus leads me and I will yield my all to Him;
I will be HIS arm extended—I'll be a Fisherman of Men.

OUR DESTINY'S PART OF YOUR PLAN

Blessed are we, who have learned to acclaim You
Who walk in the light of Your Word;
To rejoice in Your name and exalt You as king
Holding firm to the truth we have heard!
For You are our glory and strength, mighty God
You shield with Your favor and love;
Your arm is not shortened that it cannot save
Nor does Your eye ever wander from us.
Yes, Your love's forever, it will never end
And Your covenant will forever be strong;
Our hearts are established securely in You
And to You, we will FOREVER belong.
So, hide not Yourself in this hour of need
And remember Your children today;
Send forth Your angels to conquer each foe
And deliver Your people, I pray!
Praise be to You, our Lord God Forever
For You hold our lives in Your hand;
Our hopes and our dreams and our future are Yours—
And Our Destiny's Part of Your Plan!

February 4

Sweet Oasis

When I'm tossed, torn and broken, by the waves upon the sea;
When I've nothing left to offer, but the life God's given me,
May I find myself, amidst the storm, clinging to the cross;
Holding on to Jesus, and standing on the Rock!
Clothed in royal garments, protected from the storm;
Trusting in the Savior, when I am battered, tired and worn!
May my eyes turn to Jesus, where the hope of life does lie;
Clinging tightly to the cross, that speaks assurance to my mind.
When the waves are overwhelming, I'll trust upon the Lord;
To provide HIS Sweet Oasis, and calm the fiercest storm!

FEBRUARY 5

BEGINNING AND END

He is the comfort of every warm ray,
That touches our cheeks, in the light of the day.
He is the color in the sunset's glow;
That penetrates beauty, too rich to behold.
He is the fragrance, of each flower in bloom;
That dances on nostrils, with the smell of perfume.
He is the gleam, in the mist of the dew;
He's the bright shining light, of the sun and the moon.
He is the smile, that comes from within;
He's the FIRST and the LAST,
He's the—Beginning AND End!

HEART ABLAZE

Lord, Your Grace, gives me power to live a life of truth;
And Your peace guards my heart, when my focus is on You.
Even in the hard times that seem so perilous to me;
When I'm tempted, Lord, to waiver, by all the things I see.
It' when I feel so lost—and paralyzed by fear
That YOU call my name and say, "Come, My Child, up here."
For, Lord, You're forever faithful in the midst of where I am;
Giving up Your life for me, saving me from certain death.
So, Lord, may I never slumber, instead endure until the end;
Take my life and use it and guide me with Your hand.
Hold me close and keep me, when I'm facing unsure days;
Blow Your breath upon me, Lord, and set my Heart Ablaze!

HIS LIGHT UPON THE SUNRISE

I feel as if I'm crushed beneath, a heavy gruesome load;
A place where I can scarcely breathe, and love has lost its hold.
Oh, how can, I, in darkness be, where hope no longer dwells;
Alone, inside the shadows and so far outside God's realm?
Oh where, Oh where, can peace be found—how long must my
    soul wait;
Until I reach that inner core, where I am not afraid?
If only I could set my eyes, upon the Father's Heart;
And let Him gently guide me back—into His loving arms.
Could it be that in the distance, His light would shine again;
Like a beacon on an island, that would lead me back to Him?
And just maybe, in that moment, He will illuminate my eyes;
To see His love more clearly—and to KNOW, I am HIS prize!
For, I've found it's IN the struggle, of examining my soul;
That I will find my Father, and the love that His heart holds.
It's THEN, I call Him, Papa, as tears flow down my face;
And it's THERE, I find His comfort and the touch of His embrace.
And in that place of triumph, He lifts my heavy load;
He blows away the shadows and He breathes upon my soul.
For, only in His Presence, will I have eyes to see;
His Light upon the Sunrise—and ALL He's Planned for Me!

HOPE IN THE MIDST OF TRANSITION

Seasons will come and seasons will go
But there is one thing that is sure to remain;
The truth that the Lord will ALWAYS be there
In the midst of transition and change!
For Jesus is faithful to promises made—
You see, He will NEVER leave nor forsake;
Even when turmoil and fear enter in
The Holy Spirit will give peace in their place.
It's natural for man to stand and resist
Situations unfamiliar to him;
But OFTEN—it's God's hand in motion—
Bringing forth HIS divine purpose and plan.
A man's heart, MUST yield to the Spirit
And discern the sound of His voice;
When he finds himself at the fork in the road
And is faced with a difficult choice.
Finely tuned, must a man be to listen
No matter WHERE his journey may lead;
For man only sees scattered pieces—
But God sees the puzzle COMPLETE!
The Lord has so graciously given
His sweet Spirit in the core of it ALL;
He bestows Hope in the Midst of Transition
And convicts man—to stay focused on God!

FEBRUARY 9

CAPTURED FOR THE KINGDOM

I cannot change the days gone by, nor relive my life again;
But I CAN choose for TODAY, to place my life within God's
hands.
You see, He KNOWS about my yesterdays and each mistake
along the way;
Yet, He loves me just the way I am and He's given me—YET, one
more day!
I find that I am humbled—I am awestruck by His love;
There is nothing I can't accomplish, nor anything I can't give up.
He has changed me from the inside out, He has made the old
things new;
He's brought healing to my heartache—He's restored and He's
renewed.
My future lies safe in His hands because my heart belongs to
Him;
I've found that Jesus Is the Answer, He's my HOPE that dwells
within.
So, no longer will you find me, walking solely on my own;
For I've been Captured for the Kingdom—and I will NEVER walk
alone!

REST FOR MY SOUL

May I sit in Your lap
With my face on Your breast;
May You breathe upon me
And allow me to rest.
May You hold me secure
In Your loving arms;
May you fill me with hope
And keep me from harm.
May Your treasure be found
In the depth of my soul;
And may Your kindness and love
Be mine ALWAYS, to hold!
Like a child, may I come
And rest in Your peace;
Lost in the Love—
Of Your Presence So Sweet!

FEBRUARY 11

BEHIND THE VEIL

Traveling beyond limits, to a place where love prevails;
In the presence of the Lord, found Behind the Veil.
Finding priceless treasures, reserved for me alone;
As I bow my heart in honor and come before His Throne.
For it's in this place of glory where His Holy Spirit dwells;
Beyond my natural boundaries, inside HIS holy realm.
It's there my eyes are opened so I can clearly see;
His awesome hand extended, reaching out to welcome me.
Yes, it's in this place of glory where my spirit man is filled;
It's where the mysteries of God's Kingdom are so lovingly
    revealed.
It's there inside His presence, I find that I receive;
His Spirit gently wooing, as deep calls unto deep.
So, I go Behind the Veil and I seek His lovely face;
For it's there my soul is nourished and I am lost in His
    embrace.
It's there my heart is filled, inside His glory realm;
Far beyond my limitations, to a place—Behind the Veil.

To Touch the Master's Garment

The struggles I was facing, were much more than I could bear;
As I found myself upon my knees, weeping in despair.
If I could ONLY touch His garment—even JUST, its hem;
I knew that I'd be healed and truly whole again.
And then I felt His presence and His peace in such a way;
His love just seemed to saturate, as He called His saints to pray.
As I stood upon my feet, I had extraordinary strength;
For no matter what the circumstance, God was strong when I was
    weak!
He gave me light amidst the darkness and hope rooted deep
    within;
And I knew without a doubt, that I had TRULY touched His hem.

FEBRUARY 13

SHORES OF HEAVEN I'LL TROD

How can I face tomorrow's dawn,
When covered in life's blues—
How can I walk from day to day,
When I'm weary, tired and bruised?
How can I dream with hopes renewed
About a future I can't see—
When my mind is void of vision,
Of what the coming days will bring?
My only source is JESUS,
Who brings light to dreary days;
For only, HE, can lead in valleys low,
Giving hope to lead my way!
It's, HE, who gives me strength,
When I'm feeling tired and weak;
And it's, HE, who heals my broken heart
And, ALL, that bruises me!
It's JESUS who will gently lead
In the midst of trials I face;
Only, HE, can keep me going,
And hold me steady in His Grace!
And when my life is over
I'll stroll hand in hand with God;
For, I'll enter Kingdom's Glory,
And on—Heaven's Shores I'll Trod!

HIS ANCHOR ALWAYS HOLDS

Changes often bring the storms loosed to tear apart;
But in the center of the storm, I'm anchored to God's heart.
For when the storms of life sweep through, the wicked flee away;
But the righteousness of God will stand, strong and unafraid.
You see, my foundation is in Jesus—yes, He's my cornerstone;
His Word is written in my heart and I give Him place upon the
    throne.
I'll forever give Him honor, for I am awestruck of the Lord;
I'll give Him ALL, I'll ever have, in the midst of every storm.
You see, God's forever faithful in the things I cannot stop;
He provides, in spite of circumstance, for He's a loving God.
So when the storms are fierce and loosed upon my heart;
May I always find myself in Him and NOT be torn apart.
I won't despise His chastening for the Lord delights in me;
And I know when I am disciplined, it's been sent to set me free.
The very lessons He bestows will teach me in my life;
To stand strong in every storm and keep my focus upon Christ.
For when I keep my eyes on Him, my faith can't help but grow;
Yes, He's my peace within each storm and His Anchor Always
    Holds!

MIRACLES STILL HAPPEN

When we join our hearts together and pray in Jesus' name,
Miracles begin to happen and we see circumstances change.
We find, there's power in agreement when establishing God's
   truth;
Heaven's window seems to open and God begins to move.
You see, eternal power starts, within the realm of prayer,
When saints are joined together and they take the time to care.
My friend, it's time to pay attention to the burdens of the day;
Trusting God to do a miracle, standing strong and unafraid.
There will come those special times in the depth of each our lives;
To focus humbled hearts and put our trust in Christ.
For it never is too late when Jesus lives within;
To believe Him for a miracle and put our faith in Him.
I pray that many lives will change because WE take the time to
   pray
As we learn to trust in Jesus and let Him have HIS way.
Because eternal power truly starts within the realm of prayer;
And Miracles Still Happen, when we, the saints, take time to care.

*Read Acts 3: Peter and John take the time to care about a man
that is crippled, and because they do, he is healed! Silver and gold
had they none, but what they had, they gave to him. By faith the
words were spoken—rise up and walk!*

FEBRUARY 16

WE MUST PUT OUR TRUST IN JESUS FOR THE VICTORY IS THE LORD'S

The mountains may fall and crumble, into the sea that's white
    with foam;
But our God won't be surprised, nor will He shake upon His
    throne.
Instead, He watches most intently, He is NEVER unaware;
His eyes are ever watching, and He is ALWAYS there.
Our God is more than able, to break bows and shatter spears;
He's our present help in trouble, therefore, we must NOT stand
    in fear.
He is our refuge and our strength—in stillness, He is God;
We must exalt Him among the nations, and trust in Him—no
    matter what!
Our hearts must find safe shelter, beneath the covering of His
    wings;
We must rest within His shadow, and breathe the fragrance His
    peace brings.
Even in the midst of battle, inside the realm of Holy War;
We MUST trust our hearts to Jesus, and KNOW—the Victory IS
    the Lord's!

HOW MANY TIMES WILL THE FATHER BE THERE?

How many times has the Lord picked me up;
When I was broken and wounded and emotionally bankrupt?
How many times has He mended with care;
All the heartache and hurt and hopelessness there?
How many times has He soothed and caressed;
Giving strength in the midst of my weakness and stress?
What in the world could ever make me believe;
That God wouldn't be there, when I suffer and grieve?
For He'll ALWAYS be there, like He always HAS been;
To breathe upon me and heal once again!
How Many Times Will the Father Be There;
For as long as I live and have burdens to bear!

FEBRUARY 18

HIS GOODNESS, LOVE, AND MERCY

His Goodness, Love and Mercy follow me today;
Fatigue will NOT undo me, nor will I be afraid.
His love will never leave me because His Covenant is mine;
He bought me with His Blood—I'm embraced by the Divine!
Even when I feel I've failed and fallen deep in sin;
He continues to be faithful and draws me back to Him.
And though I may not understand, His mercy or His love;
His height or depth of passion or the goodness of God's Son.
His righteous still pursues me—His blessing is my cloak;
His Glory is my covering and His Mercy Is My Robe!

FEBRUARY 19

THE POTTER'S WHEEL

The vessel that was made, within the Potter's Hand;
Was marred beyond perfection—from the very fall of man.
Yet, in Him, is EVERYTHING, made to be complete;
For He sees beyond the flaws and sees what I was MEANT to be.
He takes a bit of clay and designs a masterpiece;
He makes something out of nothing and gives a second chance
    release!
You see, my God has made me over—upon the Potter's Wheel;
He gave me mercy's promise, and a masterpiece revealed!
Yes, my Father is the Potter who puts HIS Glory on Display
As He takes my life and molds it through this willing piece of
    clay!

FOCUSED ON JESUS

I'd rather be focused on Jesus today
Than hung up on riches that soon fade away.
I'd rather seek Him and the mercy He gives,
Than to rely on myself for the way I must live.
I'd rather walk daily, covered in love;
Protected by grace that comes from above.
Id rather know Jesus as Savior and Friend,
Than to journey along, and NEVER know Him!
I'd rather know Jesus and bow at His throne;
Than to compromise daily, and struggle alone.
I'd rather know Jesus than anyone else—
To be much more like Him and, LESS like myself!
I'd rather be Focused on Jesus today
With a heart that is grateful, for the price He DID pay.
I'd rather be covered in the Blood of the Lamb;
Being led by HIS purpose, HIS will and HIS plan!

FEBRUARY 21

THE DEVIL TAKES A FALL

My arsenal may not look like much
But it's more powerful than all;
For when my Father speaks for me
The Devil Takes a Fall.
I know every single circumstance
Is in my God's control;
So, it doesn't really matter
What the devil tries to throw.
His plans have been decided
In all that I'll go through;
My God is truly awesome—
He restores and He renews!
He's mighty in His Kingdom
And I WILL recover ALL;
I find that when My God Speaks FOR Me—
The Devil ALWAYS Takes a Fall.

SOMEWHERE IN THE JOURNEY

Somewhere in the Journey, there's direction for my way;
There is hope for my tomorrows and peace for each new day!
And even when I wonder, what the future days will hold;
I'll cling tightly to my dreams, my visions and my goals.
For the favor I've received, is a blessing from above;
And every talent I possess, was bestowed to me in Love!
So, I will listen for the answers, in the stillness deep within;
And I'll let His Spirit guide me, as I learn to trust in Him.
For, I know, He NEVER slumbers, He's well aware of where I've
    been;
But, HIS, purpose is much greater, than I could ever comprehend.
His hand is ALWAYS leading, in the midst of every storm;
Through confusion, doubt and fear—when I'm weary, tired and
    worn!
And Somewhere in the Journey—I will finally understand,
What it means to trust in Jesus, for HIS purpose and HIS plan!

FEBRUARY 23

GOD'S WILL PREVAILS

God chooses the least and that which seems weak;
To accomplish HIS purpose in the face of defeat.
It is going beyond all that's been known;
To that humble heart bowed at the foot of the throne!
God's now raising the level and shifting our sights
To soar beyond limits and reach higher heights.
He is calling forth warriors, those willing to fight;
To stand in the battle and watch through the night.
He's releasing anointing to those on their knees
And bestowing His power to accomplish great things.
When prayer mixes with faith, it will ALWAYS avail;
For when the heart gets involved, God's Will, WILL prevail.

His Promise of the Spring

Sometimes the ground seems rocky, hard, solid, cold and bleak;
It's impossible to fathom that life could live 'neath winter's feet.
For our eyes see only death in the season of winter's cold;
Seems life's been swallowed by the darkness and held captive by
her hold.
ONCE lovely flower beds now gone—snow's velvet blanket,
covers ALL;
No bright colors splash the canvas on the landscape's dreary wall.
The trees are bare and lifeless, the ground is littered by past
storms;
Only scars of winter's pruning are left like tattered thorns.
But still the squirrels are busy and the birds continue with their
song;
For they know that in "due" season—the harsh winter will be
gone.
For certain things are ABSOLUTE—like how the seasons come
and go;
Like the rising of the sun and the warmth within its glow.
You see, God's timing may not match our own, yet it's STILL an
absolute of truth.
For He is constant in His care for us—His love continues to stand
true.
So even when we feel the bite of winter's bitter sting;
I pray that we'll continue on and STILL have a song to sing.
God will ALWAYS bring the harvest, He's never early nor is He
late;
In due season we will surely reap if we will only stand and wait.
For God's principle of seed time and harvest can ONLY bring;
Precious fruit well worth the waiting and His Promise of the
Spring.

IMPRINTS ON THE SEASHORE

Like sand upon the seashore, there are imprints buried in;
Plain and perfect pictures, of where my life has been.
Imprints from the past, tattooed upon my heart;
Wounds that go unattended, which I am always quick to guard.
Those imprints upon my heart, have often paralyzed my life;
They've reminded me of pain, and kept me distantly from Christ.
But Jesus says the time has come, to wash the wounds away;
To cleanse the lasting imprints, that never seem to dull or fade.
To let the river from His throne, flow across the sand;
Erasing all the stubborn pictures, of who I THINK, I am!
A time to allow His Spirit, to wash and make me clean;
To flow across the imprints, and create a brand new scene.
He wants to paint a lovely portrait, on a canvas clean and smooth;
As the sand becomes a tapestry, upon which His hand can move.

Tears Are Simply Enough

A spoken farewell can NEVER convey;
What a tear from the eye can silently say.
Nor the stain on a letter, from one tear that falls;
For what a tiny tear says, will usually cover it all.
You see, when tears are released, from the depth of the soul;
They can pierce through the hurt, and bring warmth to
    console.
For, it's in a heart-splitting moment, in the midst of it all;
God will touch the emotions and let the tears fall.
Words need NOT always be spoken, to understand love;
Because sometimes in silence—Tears Are Simply Enough!

HINDS FEET FOR HIGH PLACES

Hinds Feet for High Places to rise above,
Reaching far-out extremes with more than enough.
Going higher than ever upon sharp jagged rocks
Scaling the mountain and reaching the top.
Hinds Feet for High Places, ready to climb;
Ascending to heights that others won't find.
Rising above—limitations and strife;
Surpassing each boundary, obtaining new heights.
Hinds Feet for High Places, to scale any wall;
Secure in His guidance and safe from a fall.
With revelation and wisdom to walk side by side;
Overcoming each obstacle, one at a time.
Hinds Feet for High Places, to successfully climb
The Mountain's steep path and rocky incline.

He makes my feet like the feet of deer. And sets me on
my high places.

—PSALM 18:33, NKJV

SPRING WILL PREVAIL

Revel in life's journey,
Grow not weary along your way;
Trust God to bring the springtime,
Each and every time you pray.
Sense His presence in a flower,
See the message that it brings;
Listen for HIS whisper,
In the song the sparrow sings!
Know the beauty of creation,
Share her joys and travails;
And NEVER dare forget,
Springtime WILL Prevail!

FEBRUARY 29

WALKING IN THE WAYS OF THE KINGDOM

I'm Walking in the Ways of the Kingdom
Just taking it day by day;
Listening to God's Holy Spirit
And staying close to HIS mercy and grace.
I open the door to my heart
And through obedience, follow His Will;
Then I stand and I wait for direction
And I follow the path He reveals.
It's not always to my understanding
But where He leads me, I'll go;
For I've given my ALL to Jesus
In submission, a long time ago.
So, today as I stand at the crossroads
I'm convinced, He'll show me HIS way;
I'll trust HIS light in MY darkness
To reveal the path I should take.
Yes, I'll Walk in the Ways of the Kingdom
Just taking it day by day;
I will listen to the voice of His Spirit
And trust HIM to show me the way!

Strolling with You in the Garden
Peace Within the Shadows
My Spirit Set Free
Fashion Me with Purpose
His Peace Will Calm the Winds
Arise unto a New Day
Coming to Christ in Crisis
Lay Your Ax upon the Root
Sever Not the Tie
A Warrior for the Kingdom
Wings of Freedom
One on One, Just You and Me
Sunshine Prevails
Creation's Womb
His Mercy's Sure to Keep Me
Into His Chamber
Come to the Garden
The Lover of My Soul
Bathed in His Sonshine of Peace
Journey of the Seed
Lamp unto My Soul
Expression of His Presence
It's the Journey That Counts
Light of Life
In the Silence of the Moment
God of Miracles
When the Mountains Are High
Slow Down and Take a Moment
Trail Bound for Heaven
Scars of a Broken Heart
Spotlight on My Life

MARCH

STROLLING WITH YOU IN THE GARDEN

This morning I walked in Your garden
Hand in hand, Lord, Jesus, with You;
I breathed in Your lovely fragrance
And I felt the dawn's early dew.
My heartbeat was truly captured
In the stillness of Your tender breeze;
I quieted my heart for a moment
And listened as You spoke to me.
Your Spirit brought peace and comfort
And strengthened my heart in Your love.
Lord, I find when I seek You early
I always have more than enough.
So, today as we stroll in Your garden
May the eyes of my heart become new;
As I yield to Your Holy presence
And walk hand in hand, Lord, with you!

March 2
Peace Within the Shadows

My Father watches over me, He's well aware of where I am;
Even in the midst of shadows, He holds me safely in His hands.
He assigns His angels over me, to guard me in this place;
Even though I FEEL alone—I'm still secure in His embrace.
For my God would never lead me to a place He would not be;
He'd never leave me in the shadows without the presence of His
     peace.
For my destiny is in Him—no matter what I SEE;
So, I'll look PAST my clouded vision and refuse to be deceived.
Even in the midst of shadows when the darkness seeks to scare;
And I'll rest my heart in knowing that my God is ALWAYS there.

MARCH 3

MY SPIRIT SET FREE

I know that God has kissed my soul
And set my spirit free;
I know He's summoned me to Him
And released me to receive.
To walk amidst the angels
And all He calls His own;
To enter gates of Glory
And the realm of heaven's throne.
To boldly step into a place
That far exceeds the natural eye;
Into the dominion of His Kingdom
Where He rules and reigns on high!
You see, it's ALL within my reach
Because His Spirit lives within;
He opens doors of fellowship
And sweet relationship with Him.
He draws and woos me gently
He bids me—to seek His face;
He offers me His Kingdom
In exchange for love's embrace.
And all that I must do
Is follow where He leads;
To set my heart upon Him
And trust HIS plan for me.
For He will NEVER lead me
To a place He will not be;
So I will seek Him in His Kingdom—
I'll Let Him Set My Spirit Free!

FASHION ME WITH PURPOSE

Am, I, my own worst enemy—do I falter on life's way;
Have I missed my Kingdom Purpose, like a lamb that's gone
    astray?
Do I find myself outside the fence where darkness rules the night;
In the midst of worldly shadows, in that place of compromise?
If I could only see myself through the eyes of grace and love;
Then instead of always looking down—I'd be looking UP!
Oh Lord, give me prophetic vision so I can clearly see;
My purpose in Your Kingdom and all You have for me.
Remove me from the shadows and all that overwhelms;
And thrust me into a journey, where the Holy Spirit dwells.
Lord, give me ears to hear You and eyes to see Your plan;
May I listen with my heart and guided by Your hand.
Draw me by Your Spirit that I might yield my all to You;
Father, Fashion Me with Purpose, to live my life within Your
    truth!

HIS PEACE WILL CALM THE WINDS

Does God really hear me, when I speak to calm the waves;
Has He given me authority, even when I feel afraid?
For, I've found within life's journey, I so often come across.
Tempest storms, SO violent, that bring me to the Cross.
And I cannot help but wonder, on the INSIDE of the fight;
If I really have it in me, to face the darkness of the night!
It's, THEN, I am reminded, of He, who lives in me;
The ONE who holds my life and has planned my destiny.
It's in Him, that I will make it, when I can't see past the tears;
When I'm tossed by raging winds and lost inside my fears.
I will hold on to the promise—no matter what I SEE;
Because of WHO, He is, and because He lives IN me.
I will not tuck my tail and run, when the storms of life blow in;
Instead, I'll firmly plant my feet and SPEAK, to calm the wind!
For God has given ME authority—on the INSIDE of the storm
To overcome the enemy and STAND at heaven's door!
He has promised to be with me, until the harsh winds cease;
If ONLY, I will trust Him and let HIM, give me peace.

ARISE UNTO A NEW DAY

Arise from slumbering posture
Into the season of the Lord;
Enter realms of Glory
Like you've never seen before.
Sing sweet songs of victory
And dance before His throne;
Witness heaven's splendor
And watch His prophecies unfold.
Yes, Arise unto a New Day
Receive, what's STILL beyond;
Declare the Lord's anointing
At the breaking of the dawn.
Be a signpost painted
For all the world to see;
Keep your eyes upon the heavens
And your heart upon the King!

COMING TO CHRIST IN CRISIS

I come to Christ in Crisis—I bow my heart before the Lord;
Where I'm reminded that He's carried me, so MANY times
    before.
I will give Him thanks for everything and persevere until the end;
For, He's teaching me, HIS faithfulness, and He's changing me
    within.
I've learned BEYOND each conquest, are HIS promises fulfilled;
Just waiting for His timing—to be uncovered and revealed.
You see, regardless of the circumstance, my trust MUST be in
    God;
So, I look through heaven's portal and I give Him grand applause.
I'm convinced, that He's forever faithful—yes, He is always there;
And I know, He'll guide me safely, upon the wings of prayer.
So, I will Come to Christ in Crisis—I'll bow my heart before the
    Lord;
And I'll trust Him to move mountains, just like He's ALWAYS
    done before.

LAY YOUR AX UPON THE ROOT

My heart so often struggles
With that which lies beyond control;
And my mind in anguish wanders—
Across the milestones of my soul.
This journey where I find myself
Often veers me off God's course;
Until I'm lost inside the shadows
Outside the presence of the Lord.
The darkness, like a blanket,
Comes and wraps itself so tight;
That it suffocates my being
And blinds me from the Light.
Seems I cannot find my way
To escape this pit I'm in;
Only YOU, Lord, can deliver
And renew my hope again.
Please lift this veil that covers
And turn my heart, again, to YOU;
Breathe life into my spirit—
Give me strength to stand in truth.
Shine Your Light amidst the darkness
Like a spotlight to reveal;
The pathway into Your presence
And Your loving grace that heals.
Lord, I pray that You would come
And lay Your Ax upon the Root;
Deliver me from EVERY stronghold
And all in me, that bears no fruit!

SEVER NOT THE TIE

Sever NOT the Tie, that binds me unto You;
That connects me to Your Spirit, and shows me what to do.
Sustain me through the hardships and give me eyes to see;
Where Your faithful hand is leading, and what YOU expect
    of me!
Teach me, Lord, to listen with attentive ears to hear;
Put YOUR compassion in my heart and YOUR love within
    my tears.
Help me keep my focus and give me strength within;
Until my life has ended and I reach my journey's end.
Sever NOT the Tie, that binds me to YOUR throne;
Guide me with Your hand, and safely lead me home!

A WARRIOR FOR THE KINGDOM

Rise up, oh child of God, and take your rightful place;
Put on the weapons of your warfare and gaze upon My face.
For I have called you as a warrior and I've equipped you with My shield;
I have sent a host of angels, BEFORE you on the battlefield.
Fear not in times of trouble for what your earthly eyes will see;
Instead, stand strong in battle and keep your focus upon Me.
For I will open heaven, and reveal an unseen realm;
Where angels fight the battles and bring demonic forces down.
Yes, you will know My power and fight within My strength;
As anointing pours upon you from your head down to your feet.
YOU will witness miracles, and see with your own eyes;
Signs and wonders set before you, beneath the hole in heaven's sky.
Yes, YOU, My child are called, for such a time as this;
To be a Warrior for the Kingdom, to stand and fight for righteousness.
The battlefield's before you, so COME and take your place;
Put on the weapons of your warfare and pick up the shield of faith.

MARCH 11

WINGS OF FREEDOM

High upon the treetop, I saw a tiny nest
Filled with baby sparrows, perched for final test.
You see, today would be the day to leave their twig-filled home;
And take a leap of faith, unto the great unknown.
One by one they fluttered and stretched their wings to fly;
Dotting earth's horizon upon the canvas of the sky.
Each had found their way to fly upon the wind;
To go beyond the boundaries of where their tiny nest had been.
God's hand had lifted them and He taught them how to fly;
He blew His breath upon them and released them to the sky.
If God takes so much care, to teach a sparrow how to fly
How much MORE will He do, concerning you and I?
You see, His eye is ever watchful, we will never be alone
Even when He calls our faith to step into the great unknown.
For He is always faithful to give us wings to fly;
Far beyond our every boundary, across the canvas of His sky.
He blows His breath upon us, He gives us ride upon His wind;
And He carries us to places that we have never been.
In Him, there are no limits concerning you and I;
Only Wings of Freedom, to soar beyond His highest heights!

ONE ON ONE, JUST YOU AND ME

It's not what I can do OR not
That qualifies my life;
It's when I Fall upon the Rock
And cling with all my might.
For it's only in Your presence
That I am truly moved;
It is NEVER in performance—
Of what I can OR cannot do!
It's when I find YOUR treasure
Hidden deep within my soul;
A gift that has no measure—
Nor boundaries in its hold.
It's Your awesome love, Lord Jesus
That You so freely share with me;
As I come into Your presence
And humbly yield on bended knee.
For it's ME, You seek to find
Not the THINGS that I can DO;
It's my heart that You are after
And so lovingly pursue.
So today I Fall upon the Rock—
It's the ONLY place for me;
In the presence of the Living God
One on One, Just You and Me!

MARCH 13

SUNSHINE PREVAILS

When you walk through the valley, Jesus is there;
To give comfort and love, mercy and care.
He'll never leave you alone, in the midst of the storm;
Even when you FEEL, battered, weary and worn.
He sees every hurt, pain and heartache in you;
He wants to heal and restore, He wants to touch and renew.
But half of the battle is sharing the grief;
That is hidden within, where eyes cannot see.
To admit in your heart, that you've suffered great loss;
And to bring every sorrow, to the foot of the cross.
So, dark shadows MAY come, and you may think God's failed;
But when the storm's over, you'll see His work unveiled.
And someday you'll know, God's GREAT plan for you;
In the midst of the suffering and all you've been through!

CREATION'S WOMB

There's nothing quite like
The sweet smell of spring;
Nor the echoes of life
And beauty it brings.
For nature responds
By coming alive;
Unfolding with grace
In amazing surprise.
It's the heart of the Father
Confirming His love;
It's life's sweet creation
That blossoms and buds.
For each bloom of a flower
And chirp the bird sings;
Reminds us that Jesus
Is alive in ALL things.
It's His way of expressing
That death CANNOT win;
It's the mystery of nature
That God ALWAYS sends.
It's God's glory and splendor
Portrayed in full bloom;
It's His grandeur expanding
From Creation's Own Womb!

MARCH 15

HIS MERCY'S SURE TO KEEP ME

When the rhyme has lost its reason, and the flower sheds its
   bloom;
When the morning sunrise ceases, and only darkness fills the
   room.
When hope evades reality, and life has lost its song;
When nothing's in its place, and everything seems wrong.
It's then, my heart looks upward toward the shining SON;
Engulfing HIS sweet promise, to NOT leave anything, undone.
For even in this season, of devastation and remorse;
I will put my trust in Jesus and let Him keep my life on course.
You see, there will always be SOME things that I will not
   understand;
But I've built my life upon the Rock—not on the sinking sand!
So, as long as I have breath, I will never turn away;
From the one that I call Savior, and His All-Consuming Grace.
Yes, He has heard my cries, from the depth of deep despair;
And He has sent His comfort, upon the Wings of Prayer.
His Mercy's Sure to Keep Me and His Love, Is Sure to Hold,
My heart inside the darkness and the anguish of my soul.
He will never leave me—nor forsake me in this place;
Instead, He'll pick me up, and hold me close, in HIS embrace!

MARCH 16

INTO HIS CHAMBER

Oh, Lord, I come into Your chamber with nothing more upon my
   mind;
Than to yield my humble heart, and see You, ONLY, as Divine!
Even in the midst of chaos, when the storms are swirling round;
I will take the time to come and in Your presence, bow!
As I see the royal scepter extended from Your hand;
I will dive into the DEEP and respond to Your command.
You require of me, Oh Lord, to be washed inside Your love;
To trust You with my ALL, and by faith, just merely come.
Your treasures lie before me, in this place You've called me to;
So I lock my eyes upon You, no matter WHAT I'm going through.
I come into Your presence and Your holiness pursue;
Where my heart is cleansed in beauty and my spirit man
   renewed.
There is nothing in the world, more incredible than You;
Your Grace Is ALL Sufficient, and Your Mercies Always New!
So, it's into Your Chamber, Lord, that my heart finds its home;
The place of Your dwelling, before heaven's throne!

MARCH 17

COME TO THE GARDEN

Lord, can we Come to the Garden and talk for awhile;
Can we rest and refresh, before we begin the next mile?
You see, the journey is long and the race is intense;
And I need just a moment, to be still and sit!
I need to relax in Your presence, and drink in your wonderful
    peace;
Where the cares of this world are diminished, and all of my
    worries cease!
I need to find Your refreshment, and strength so I can go on;
I need to ponder on, YOU, for awhile—the one where my help
    comes from.
I need to breathe in, Your hope, and rest in Your arms of love;
I just need some personal time with YOU, until my tank, is filled
    up!
So, today, I Come to the Garden, to spend quiet time with YOU;
To find rest when my life is chaotic—in a place where my spirit's
    renewed!

THE LOVER OF MY SOUL

Your love is like the rushing waves
upon the shoreline of my soul;
Drawing me to greater depths
than my heart has ever known.
It's as if, Oh Lord, You've swallowed up
all that's not of You;
And set Your eyes upon me—
with love's passion to pursue.
It's like I'm drawn into Your presence
in a secret place where we're alone;
Where I'm showered with sweet fragrance
that can only come from heaven's throne.
It's then my heart is overcome
in the glory of it all;
To KNOW the Lover of My Soul
is the awesome Son of God.
Just to think—YOU are my bridegroom
and I'm Your lovely bride;
Goes far beyond my comprehension
or the thoughts within my mind.
For NOW, my eyes see dimly
the love that Your heart holds;
And I have to steal away the TIME—
for us to be alone.
But one day soon on heaven's shore
the veil will be removed;
As I become the lovely bride
who comes to join her waiting groom.
It's then my heart will know ALL truth
as I enter heaven's door;
As I bow to love's sweet passion—
in the presence of the Lord

Yes, I'll be drawn to greater depths
than my heart has ever known;
And I will humbly yield my ALL
to the Lover of My Soul.

BATHED IN HIS SONSHINE OF PEACE

To be like a watered garden
Whose spring will never fail;
To bask in the Sonshine of Glory
And drink from the Father's Well.
To listen intently in silence
As the fluttering bird sings her song;
To hear heaven's melody upward—
To know that His Coming's not long!
To quiet my soul in His presence
And submit to HIS ultimate plan;
To FEEL, the warmth, of His Spirit
And the majesty of His hand.
To be completely filled and enveloped
By the washing of marvelous grace;
To breathe in the breath of His fragrance
And be wrapped in His arms of embrace.
To be carried on the wings of angels
And placed at the Master's Feet;
To worship in the light of His Glory
And Bathed in His Sonshine of Peace!

MARCH 20

JOURNEY OF THE SEED

The tiny seeds are planted, so, NOW, we sit and wait;
We do not know the final journey, each tiny seed will take.
We can only hope for fertile ground, so the tiny seeds can grow;
We can only plant and water, but the FINAL outcome is
   unknown.
So, we prepare the ground and plant, then we water and we weed;
We do ALL we know to do, to protect the tiny seeds.
But we can only do SO much, and then our part is finally done;
We must trust the process of the journey, which has only just
   begun.
The journey that the seed will take, is NOT within OUR hands;
And the outcome of the journey, is often hard to understand.
For there are always outside forces, that threaten the tiny seeds;
From the time that they are planted, until fruition is complete.
But the outcome of the journey, will surely take its course;
When we've done all we know to do—THEN we just wait and
   trust the Lord.
For ONLY Jesus knows the outcome, of every tiny seed we plant;
And the process of its journey, even when we fail to understand.
So, trust HIM with the process, of the Journey of the Seed;
From the time that it is planted, until the harvest is complete!

MARCH 21

LAMP UNTO MY SOUL

Beauty fades before my eyes—but grace FOREVER holds;
It won't diminish in the night—for it's a Lamp unto My Soul!
It's who I am in times alone, when only I can see
The calloused edges marked by time, and know I'm truly free.
It's grace that keeps me in His care but it's my lifestyle lived in
    Him
That draws me to the throne of God and fills me up within.
It's knowing Christ as Savior, deep within my soul;
It's peace in knowing I'm in Him and never letting go.
Yes, beauty fades before me—but grace FOREVER holds;
It won't diminish in the night—for it's a Lamp unto My Soul!

MARCH 22

EXPRESSION OF HIS PRESENCE

It's the Expression of His Presence alive within my soul;
It's the beauty of His holiness that draws me to His throne.
It's the Spirit of the Lord that causes me to fly;
For He's the wind beneath my wings on which I soar to higher
    heights.
He's untied my every anchor that has tried to hold me down;
And He's lifted me to rise above and go to higher ground.
He's placed a hunger in my heart and a thirsting in my soul;
He's released me in His Kingdom to come before His throne.
It's there my soul is nourished and filled beyond its brim;
It's bowing in His presence and making time for Him.
It's there I find communion reserved for me alone;
For in the presence of the Lord, I've found sweet favor at His
    throne.
He's the Alpha and Omega, the Beginning and the End
He's the treasure my heart holds and I'll forever live in Him.

It's the Journey That Counts

It's the Journey That Counts, on life's rocky road;
It's the pearls found within, that are being exposed.
It's the passion and love, of exploring life's dream;
And finding true meaning, in small minute things!
It's the vision to see, through the eyes of the heart;
The REAL meaning to life, while looking through scars!
It's the Journey That Counts, as life's race is run;
Keeping eyes upon Jesus—until the battles are won!

LIGHT OF LIFE

Entrenched within my heart, is sweet assurance that God sees;
That He is watching very closely and hears my every plea.
And the very day I call for help, the tide of battle turns;
My enemies reverse and flee—my supplications HAVE been
    heard!
I am trusting in the Lord, I put my confidence in Him;
I know His promises are true, and every answer, He, will send.
God is for me, not against me—this one thing, I know for sure;
So I will trust Him for the outcome, no matter WHAT, I must
    endure!
He keeps my feet from stumbling and He helps me walk upright;
Because my focus is on Jesus—the only one true light!

MARCH 25

IN THE SILENCE OF THE MOMENT

In the Silence of the Moment, she could hear her heartbeat stop;
It's as if all time were over—with no more ticks, upon the clock.
Reality was crashing in, and where was she to turn;
How could she find the answers, if she refused to learn?
In the Silence of the Moment, she saw herself so weak;
How could she face another day, without some inner strength?
Dependent for so many years, upon HERSELF, in life;
She never really felt the NEED, to turn her heart to Christ!
But in the Silence of the Moment, she bowed her heart in prayer;
She gave her heart to Jesus, along with every sin and care!
Suddenly, her heart was filled, with an overwhelming peace,
And she began to rise ABOVE, with extraordinary strength!
In the Silence of the Moment, her life was changed forevermore;
Because she rolled her burdens over, upon the shoulders of the
    Lord.
From that day on, she trusted Him, to lead her through each day;
To overcome her struggles and the trials in her way.
For, in the Silence of the Moment, the Lord did gently speak;
He breathed His breath upon her, and He filled her with HIS
    peace!

GOD OF MIRACLES

You, Lord, have the power, to send a miracle my way;
For in You, there are NO limits, only answers when I pray.
Yes, some things in this life are just reserved for You, alone;
Like the awesome gift of healing that flows from heaven's throne.
Lord, YOU have the ability, to give back what I have lost
And the method of my miracle rests within YOUR hands, Oh
    God.
So, in times when I'm exposed for all the world to see;
May I humbly come before You and present to You, my need.
For I know that something happens within the Spirit realm
When I come in true humility and lay my burdens down.
So, today, my heart IS humbled as Your mercy I pursue
Lord, I thank You in advance and give all the glory unto YOU!
For You ARE a God of Miracles and there's nothing You can't do
I believe that YOU are awesome and Your promises are TRUE!

When the Mountains Are High

There are times in the climb, when I want to STOP;
When the mountain's too steep and I cannot SEE God!
There's a moment of choice, when, BY FAITH, I must see;
I am NEVER alone and, God will NEVER leave me!
Even in weariness, when the mountain seems HIGH;
I will trust and obey, and continue to climb.
For God instills courage, He gives strength to my faith;
When I choose to believe and let HIM lead the way.
So, I will trust Him today, when I want to give up;
And I'll continue to climb, even though it seems rough!

SLOW DOWN AND TAKE A MOMENT

Slow Down and Take a Moment—Remember, WHO, You Are;
You're just a human being, with a very HUMAN heart!
It's a heart that sometimes hurts, and a heart that carries pain;
A heart consumed by pressure, from unwanted stress and strain.
So, it's time to take a moment, far from struggles that you FEEL;
And let God blow His breath on you—to nurture, soothe and
 heal!
Let Him take, with tender love, your heart within HIS hands;
And immerse you in His Spirit, breathing life in you again!
Give Him every circumstance, that was meant to bring you pain;
And place them on HIS shoulders, even though it may feel
 strange!
For, He's just waiting for the moment, when your heart will truly
 yield;
To the suffering of emotions and the heartache that you FEEL!
So, Slow Down and Take a Moment—Remember, WHO, You
 Are;
And Let God bring some comfort, to your tired and weary heart!

TRAIL BOUND FOR HEAVEN

The rebel walks a treacherous road, that's thorny all the way;
But a man who values his OWN soul, will seek Christ to lead his
way.
For the path that's set before you, has MANY twists and turns;
And there is wisdom in direction, and rewards for each thing
learned.
And it takes real understanding, to walk from mile to mile;
On the pathway set before you, full of hardships, storms and
trials.
But the man who walks with Jesus, and takes courage for his soul;
Will be on a Trail Bound for Heaven, and NOT a treacherous
road!

SCARS OF A BROKEN HEART

Hidden deep beneath the surface, where the human eye can't go;
There is often pain and suffering and the sting of past sorrow.
It never seems to cease, it's like a faithful loyal friend;
Always there reminding you, of all the pain within.
The ONLY hope of restoration is to know God's Word is TRUE;
To gain strength within HIS power, each day to make it through!
For, HE, sees the inner pain, that no one else can see;
He knows the anguish of the heart, and hears every desperate
  plea!
He offers rest in times of weariness, and opens blinded eyes;
Revealing Himself, as faithful, to heal the brokenness of life.
It's Him, and ONLY Him, that can be trusted to stand guard;
To take away, past sorrow, and heal—the Scars of a Broken Heart!

SPOTLIGHT ON MY LIFE

I don't always have the answers,
Nor do I pretend to understand;
But I know the ONE who holds the key
To ALL my future plans!
At times, I cannot comprehend,
And I often feel so weak;
But it's, THEN, He lifts me up on high
And fills me with HIS strength.
He carries me through battles
That I can't even see;
He delivers me from circumstance
And the deceitful enemy!
He was there from the beginning
And He'll remain until the end;
He has His Spotlight on My Life
And His Spirit lives within.
So, my future IS secure,
No matter, WHAT, I face;
Because His Spotlight's on My Life
And I am covered, by His Grace!

APRIL

He Quiets My Soul
New Mercies for Each Day
A God Chaser
At the Sound of His Thunderous Roar
Heaven's Crown Will Forever Be Mine
Overcomer's Reward
Leaning on Love
In Him I'm Secure
You Know Where I Am
The Shepherd's Love
Hope Restored
Quiet My Heart and Bring Peace to My Soul
His Word Is My Promise
Believing for a Miracle
The Father's Gentle Whisper
Strength Within the Storm
The Glory of His Presence
Mystery of His Faithfulness
Walking in the Favor
Just Reward
Remember Whose Side You're On
Heavenly Realm of Battle
Endless Treasures
Gifts Within Me
Good Shepherd
He's the Hope of My Faith
Simply Believe
Champion of God
Walking Daily in His Love
The Skies of Dawn

April 1

He Quiets My Soul

He Quiets My Soul, in the cool of the day
Where the breeze calmly blows and the trees gently sway.
Where morning breaks forth and its light lifts my eyes;
To the brilliance and splendor of heaven's blue skies.
Where sweet harmony sings and beckons me—"Come"
To the light of the world—to the heart of God's Son.
Where grace lovingly covers my head to my toes
Where the touch of His hand, truly quiets my soul.
To a place where His whisper, is all I can hear
And the brush of His hand, wipes away every tear.
Where my troubles and trials, yield to the light
Where my spirit man flies and reaches new heights.
Yes, in the presence of Jesus, unfailing mercy unfolds
His breath breathes forth life—and He Quiets My Soul!

NEW MERCIES FOR EACH DAY

His mercy flows from heaven
It heals, restores, renews;
It's consistent EVERY day
Much like the morning dew!
His compassion NEVER fails
Nor does He turn His ear away;
You see, Faithful is my Father
With New Mercies for Each Day!
He alone's my portion
He's the hope within my soul;
He holds my heart FOREVER—
He will NEVER let it go.
His mercy is ALWAYS new
Every Morning—Every Day;
Sent upon the breath of Jesus
To wash the world away.
He covers me with love—
Unfailing mercy without end;
EVERY day—His mercy's new
Time and Time Again!

APRIL 3

A GOD CHASER

A heart that chases after God will catch Him in the end;
For the one who seeks His face, will come to know Him as a
friend.
They won't just know ABOUT Him, and all that He can give;
Instead they'll know the person—for WHO He truly is!
Their hearts are like small children who chase after and pursue;
They're looking for a Father's arms to safely run into.
With eyes completely focused upon the ONE in whom they
chase;
They know that they must catch Him to truly see Him face to
face.
They want to apprehend His presence and encounter life with
Him:
To catch His heart, like David, and truly call Him—Friend!
A heart that chases after God will comprehend the depth of love;
They'll find their hunger satisfied and truly know He IS enough!
For the one who runs with passion and pursues God face to face;
Will find his OWN self captured within the Father's warm
embrace!

AT THE SOUND OF HIS THUNDEROUS ROAR

Deep in the depths of affliction
I can hear a distant roar;
It rumbles on my spirit's horizon
Shouting the Word of the Lord!
For the bowels of hell cannot keep me
Tethered in chains anymore;
Because, HE, that is living within me
Is upright and He's beginning to ROAR!
The Lion of Judah emerges
In Glory and Strength and Power;
The defeat of the enemy surges
And fades like a withering flower.
The light of God's marvelous Kingdom
Has appeared in the Father's Own Son;
Triumphant is HE for the ages
And in Him, EVERY victory, is won!
The Lion's now taken position
To stand guard o'er my life, evermore;
I can smell the breath from His nostrils
And I can HEAR the sound of His Roar!
All of the earth, NOW, is shaking
For His entrance is so close at hand;
Soon we will see His appearing
And know—He's the Great I Am!
So, today, may my spirit man listen
With an ear finely tuned to the Lord;
May the hope in my heart be ignited,
At the Sound of His Thunderous Roar!

HEAVEN'S CROWN WILL FOREVER BE MINE

Earth's cross, that I bear, last a moment,
But Heaven's Crown Will Forever Be Mine;
It has radiance, splendor and purpose
That cannot be tarnished by time.
It's the Realm of the Father's Glory
The hope of the ages to come;
Where death is not swallowed by darkness
And men live by the light of the Son.
It's the shoreline that marks my FOREVER
A place of no turning back;
Where the blessings of God are poured forth
In abundance, without any lack.
Yes, it's the Realm of the Father's Glory
It's His every promise fulfilled
Where Grace is the air's sweet aroma
And lush is the grass in the field.
Yes, the hope of my every tomorrow—
Eternity's home for all time;
NOW, the cross that I bear, last a moment
But Heaven's Crown Will Forever Be Mine!

OVERCOMER'S REWARD

Sometimes within the struggle, I cannot always feel;
The presence of His Spirit or the truth that HE reveals.
I know, by FAITH, He's with me, and that I am not alone;
But, at times, I feel so helpless, completely blind and without
     hope!
Emotions are such funny things, they make us laugh or cry;
They give peace to face the future, or give fear to run and hide.
My emotions are God Given, but sometimes I can't control;
The effects they have upon me, or their strength upon my soul.
By faith, my heart is beckoned, to push PAST, the things I FEEL;
Into the presence of His Spirit and the TRUTH that He reveals.
For, He leads me through each trial, with His strength to
     overcome;
In the midst of WHERE I am, until the victory has been won!
So, I've found that in each struggle, it doesn't matter how I FEEL;
As long as I am focused, upon what I KNOW, is REAL!

LEANING ON LOVE

Carried away by the dream of it all;
Standing aloof from the presence of God.
Watching and waiting, expecting to see;
Each selfish desire, truly holding the key.
And then just like that, I realized success;
Is not measured by money, good looks or fine dress.
But its value is found, where the heart is sincere;
Unselfish and kind, always ready to hear.
Listening for answers that come from above;
Trusting by faith and Leaning on Love.

APRIL 8

IN HIM I'M SECURE

When I walk in a place unfamiliar
It's so easy to stumble and fall;
My feet feel unsure in the journey
And my eyes try to wander from God.
But my heart's roots grow deep in Jesus
So I know I will make it through
All I can do in the process
Is continue to focus on truth!
You see, Jesus ALONE is my refuge
And my rock in the midst of the storm;
I need ONLY remember each promise
And steady myself in the Lord.
For He is the answer in ALL things—
No matter WHERE my journey leads;
He has established His purpose and plan
And He lays out the pathway for me.
I may not always see clearly
But I'll continue to quiet my soul;
To listen intently to Jesus
And walk where He leads me to go.
So even when life becomes awkward
And my steps tend to feel so unsure;
I will turn my heart toward heaven
And KNOW that in Him, I'm Secure.

You Know Where I Am

Lord, I'm so easily distracted by the things of this world;
My heart is in turmoil and my mind's in a whirl.
I can't seem to find my way to Your throne;
I'm lost in the journey and feeling alone.
I need You so much to come rescue and save;
To let heaven's mercy, be poured out like rain.
Please hear me, Oh Father, surround me today;
Let me rest in Your strength and Your sweet loving grace.
Help me stop wandering and stumbling along;
Give me meaning and purpose and my life a new song!
I need You to find me more than anything else;
For I know I will die if I'm left to myself.
I cannot keep going the way I am now;
So I'll stop in my steps and I'll wait here awhile.
I KNOW that You'll come and find this lost lamb;
For You care about me and You Know Where I Am!

APRIL 10

THE SHEPHERD'S LOVE

God's eyes are always scanning
He is looking to and fro;
He's calling forth HIS sheep
And dividing them from goats.
You see, True sheep WILL hear the voice
Of the Shepherd when He calls;
They'll be drawn to Him in safety
As they seek the hem of God.
For OUTSIDE His protection
They are vulnerable and weak;
But they find they're most secure
When resting at His feet.
For anything that seeks to harm
Must first pass the Shepherd's way;
And because He stands on guard
The sheep are not afraid.
They are hopelessly devoted
To the one who watches them;
They trust Him with their lives
And keep their eyes on Him.
True sheep will trust their Shepherd
They will follow where He leads;
They will rest within His shadow
And find their shelter at His feet.
For within His peaceful presence
They find they always have enough;
They've been captured by contentment
Within the Shepherd's Love!

APRIL 11

HOPE RESTORED

Is there a place to run away—a spot to safely hide;
Where the shadows cannot follow and the darkness cannot find?
Is there life within the reason—far from ALL that's after me;
Can faith unlock a season and point me to my destiny?
Could I come beneath the wing of my Father's loving arms;
And find peace inside His presence, to keep me safe from harm?
When the hope inside my heart, has been deferred AGAIN;
Will I trust Him in the pit, of where I find I am?
Can I believe that if I Ask, I'll Get—and if I Seek, I'll Find;
Can I know that if I choose to KNOCK—He'll open EVERY time?
For, you see, sometimes, I grow weary and often lose the will to
  fight;
It's like the darkness seems to hover, like a fog upon the night.
I wish that I could just shake loose and be free to truly fly;
Far past this earth's horizon, into the star-filled sky.
To KNOW that God will keep me, in the solace of His care;
When I look to Him for answers and BELIEVE that He'll be there.
So, when the darkness eases in, and steals my will to fight;
I will ASK until I GET—and I will SEEK until I FIND.
I will KNOCK until He OPENS—and then I'll enter through the
  door;
Where HIS light, becomes my beacon—and My HOPE, Becomes
  Restored!

> Hope deferred makes the heart sick, But when the desire
> comes, it is a tree of life.
>
> —PROVERBS 13:12, NKJV

APRIL 12

QUIET MY HEART AND BRING PEACE TO MY SOUL

Lord, calm me within
To the depth of my soul;
Show me my worth
And the value I hold.
Give me Your ear
To hear and obey;
Your plan for my life
Today and Always!
Touch my blind eyes
And cause them to see;
My journey, in You,
That lies before me.
Fill every void
Every crevasse and hole
Lord, Quiet My Heart
And Bring Peace to My Soul.

HIS WORD IS MY PROMISE

God taught me to fly on the wings of His Word
To hold on by faith to all I have heard.
He gave me His promise to ALWAYS be there
In the midst of each trial and depth of despair.
He gave me His Word as a two-edged sword
To pierce through the darkness and do battle in war.
Against all the odds I've stood and I've fought
I've seen miraculous victories at the Hand of my God.
So, I'll continue my journey—sometimes weary and beat
Because Jesus calls me to triumph, NOT to defeat!
Yes, His Word IS My Promise and it lives within me
So I'll trust and I'll follow even when I feel weak.
For God has taught me to fly on the wings of His Word
To reach beyond limits and soar like a bird.
You see, my life's in His hands, my heart's at His feet
His Word IS My Promise and He Is My Strength!

APRIL 14

BELIEVING FOR A MIRACLE

When it comes, Lord, to receiving
Miracles from YOU;
May I find that I'm positioned
To be touched, filled and renewed.
Let me stand before You—
Aware of who You are;
Face to Face with Glory
Connected—Heart to Heart!
May my faith NOT waiver
Instead, Lord, help me stand;
Trusting YOU—for the impossible
In the midst of where I am.
Yes, I'm Believing for a Miracle
My eyes are fixed on YOU;
Lord, I've put my heart in Your hands—
And my faith will not be moved!

APRIL 15

THE FATHER'S GENTLE WHISPER

It's my Father's Gentle Whisper,
Riding in upon the breeze;
That calms the fiercest storms,
That rage inside of me.
It's His hand of peace that touches
And soothes my weary soul;
When I'm lost inside the shadows—
In that place of no control.
It's the hope He freely offers
To the turmoil in my life;
When I've given in to pressures
And dreadful doubts that plague my mind!
It's that tender, subtle, whisper,
Piercing depths I cannot see;
As my Father calms the waters
And releases peace in me.
It's knowing He is there,
To calm my every storm;
When the harsh winds blow their fury
And I can hear the thunderous roar.
It's trusting He will come
When I call upon His name,
It's building faith in Jesus
When all I feel is pain!
It's listening for HIS whisper,
That rides in upon the breeze;
It's giving Him my EVERYTHING,
No matter what I SEE!

APRIL 16

STRENGTH WITHIN THE STORM

Tossed amidst the raging storm and waves upon the sea;
Lost inside the waters—completely covering me!
I cried, "Oh Lord, come help me" and He lifted me on high;
He raised me up, inside the storm, and gave me wings to fly!
I find that I can trust Him, to come and calm the winds;
When I feel I'm going under, with no hope to rise again!
Yes, even in the roughest winds and waves upon the sea;
He is MORE than able, to come and rescue me.
There is peace to rise above, when I call unto the Lord;
For He calms the raging waters,
And gives me—Strength Within the Storm!

APRIL 17

THE GLORY OF HIS PRESENCE

There is no situation, that I will be in;
That doesn't give purpose and a reason to live.
For I was created to walk in a plan;
And there's no circumstance that will change who I am!
I will only see greatness, when I'm doing God's Will;
Because HE'S given me purpose and specific plans to fulfill.
You see, there is a place, where I am never alone;
It's in the presence of Jesus—at the foot of His Throne!
It's there, in that Glory, that my heart surely knows;
HIS purpose and plan of where He's called me to go!

APRIL 18

MYSTERY OF HIS FAITHFULNESS

The Mystery of His Faithfulness, lie's within His Holy Name;
His promise is the breath, in which my future is contained.
My covenant with Jesus, will lead me every day;
Through trials and tribulations, upon my journey's way!
He never makes a promise, that's He's unequipped to keep;
He is the one who called me, and it's HE, who gives me strength.
It's He, who works within me, to make me who I am;
Only, HE, can make the way, and shape me from within.
He's present in the promise, and He creates for me;
The purpose of my future and HIS reality!
Faith and Hope will move me, into a treasured life;
When I find that I am grounded and my identity's in Christ.
He called me to Himself, and HIS covenant was made;
It's the Mystery of His Faithfulness and His Overwhelming Grace!

WALKING IN THE FAVOR

I know what I'm going after—yes, I've a definite target in mind;
You see, MY destiny follows direction, of all that is rightfully
mine.
My past will never affect me, for I'm now clean and I've left it
behind
I'm no longer walking in bondage, instead, I now have the
courage to climb.
The anointing of God falls upon me, it covers from my head to
my toes;
You see, my attitude tends to soar upward, when I walk in the
things that I know.
I'm always prepared for tomorrow and I'm continually ready to
change
I'm walking, where the Lord calls me—in the flow of His
marvelous grace.
Yes, I'm moving within His favor, for I walk in the favor of God;
Even though, at times, it's contrary, to whether I'll make it or not.
I will get to the place and I'll wait, for the hand of the Lord within
Yes, He'll open the door to my future, as I put all my trust in Him.
I find that I'm in His favor, and all that He has is mine;
HE possesses the key to my future and HE, holds the hands of
time.

APRIL 20

JUST REWARD

Never let life's enemy, rob your passion or your zeal;
For God has made you salt upon the earth, and a light upon the
    hill!
Never lose your confidence, lest you lose your Just Reward;
Have courage for God's promises, and hold tightly to the Lord.
Accept the truth that faces you, yield yourself to do HIS will;
Friend, don't give up your faith, no matter HOW you FEEL.
You need to know you're value, when Jesus looks at you
You need to be encouraged and KNOW you'll make it through!
So, cast not away your confidence, nor your trust upon the Lord;
For, when it's all been said and done—You'll Receive Your Just
    Reward!

April 21

Remember Whose Side You're On

When the Cross was prepared for Jesus
Do you think the devil had a clue
That the part he'd play—would actually be,
For God, the GREATEST thing he'd EVER do!
You see, Satan covered the world in darkness
He blinded the eyes of men;
He mocked the death of Jesus
And he considered it the END!
But what he never took time to realize
When he stood in pride to gloat;
Was this path was NOT his own—
It was predestined from Heaven's Throne!
Never once did Satan have domain
Nor have victory in the land;
Even Christ's Death upon the Cross
Was designed by God's Own Plan!
So, we must take an account of WHO God IS
And NOT focus with worldly eyes;
For there's NOTHING the devil will ever do
That will catch God by surprise.
The final victory is ALREADY determined—
YES, God will ALWAYS Win;
His righteousness WILL surely prevail—
He's the Beginning—He's the End!
So, when we're surrounded by the darkness
And it appears the devil's won;
May God remind us of the CROSS
And Whose Side We're Really On!

HEAVENLY REALM OF BATTLE

The heavenly battle rages on, in a realm I cannot see;
But God has sent a host of angels, to stand and fight for me!
My eyes can't SEE the battle, but nonetheless, the battle's real;
And I find that I'm the target, upon the battlefield!
Unleashed are powers of darkness, assigned with chaos for my
    life;
Sent to kill, steal and destroy, because I belong to Christ.
BUT, the devil's days are numbered, he knows he CANNOT win;
For the God of ALL Creation, WILL have the Victory in the end!
So for NOW the battle rages, in a realm that's still unseen;
As an army of God's angels, come to stand and fight for me.
You see, God sees me as HIS treasure, I belong to HIM, alone;
And the depth of Hades' reach, has NOT the power to take God's
    Own!

ENDLESS TREASURES

How can I capture this moment in time,
When I'm not even sure, it was meant to be mine?
Was it a fluke that just happened to be,
Or was it God's plan, from the beginning for me?
For whatever the reason, I will grasp and take hold
Of the blessings from heaven that seem to unfold
And when it's all over—when it's all said and done,
I'll sit back and relax in the love of God's Son!
I'll breathe in the fragrance, of His cool gentle breeze,
Overwhelmed by the moment and all that I see.
For His Treasures Are Endless, His Mercy's Are New—
His Love Is Forever and His Word ALWAYS, True!
He's written my name in the palm of His Hand,
He's molded my life to BE, who I am!
So, I'll not take for granted, what was meant to be mine
And I'll capture this moment, that's been marked out in
    time!
I won't be discouraged, I'll watch and I'll wait—
Because time's in HIS hand, and He's NEVER late!
His Treasures Are Endless, His Mercy's Are New—
His Love Is Forever, and His Word, ALWAYS, True!

APRIL 24

GIFTS WITHIN ME

May the gifts You have given
And placed within me;
Be used for YOUR Glory,
To satisfy needs.
For I know there are things
That you've called me to do,
You have made me unique,
And prepared me for You!
You've anointed me, Lord,
And deposited seed;
So, that I could fulfill,
What You've planned for me.
My heart is to walk
In the midst of my call;
With eyes that are focused
On a pathway to God!
So, I give you my gifts—
Come and do as You choose;
Lord, Fill me and use me
And make me like You!

April 25

Good Shepherd

Jesus, the Good Shepherd, is always by your side;
For He protects and watches over, He loves and gently guides!
His lambs are MOST important, so they never need to fear;
For, Jesus, the Good Shepherd, is always close when danger's
    near!
His grace is ALL sufficient, to meet any need that comes;
He defeats your every enemy, and causes them to run!
There is NOTHING you will face, that will catch Him unaware;
And He is MORE than able, to expose the devil's snare!
Yes, Jesus the Good Shepherd, is ALWAYS by your side;
He protects and watches over—He loves and gently guides!

APRIL 26

HE'S THE HOPE OF MY FAITH

My spirit is fueled
By each promise Christ gives;
And I find my hope is increased
When I keep my eyes upon Him.
Yes, hope fills my soul
From bottom to top;
It's the anchor that holds
Me securely to God.
Hope is His love
Lavished freely upon me;
It's the Holy Spirit's deposit—
The Father's own guarantee.
You see, I am God's child
No matter WHAT comes my way;
So I won't let my hope
Be snatched or stolen away.
My heart is fixed upon Jesus
And I will NOT be swayed;
You see, I know without doubt—
He's the Hope of My Faith!

SIMPLY BELIEVE

Lord, if I could hear Your voice in the whisper of my ear;
I would sincerely listen, and make sure that I could hear.
If I could smell Your fragrance as it rides upon the breeze;
I'd capture its aroma and let it be the air I breathe.
If I could feel Your touch upon the sands of time;
I'd be a lot more patient and trust YOUR will not mine.
If I could see Your grandeur upon the mountaintop
I would open up my eyes and know for sure, You are my God.
If I could taste Your goodness in the harvest time so sweet
I would open up my mouth and I would surely eat.
If I could only understand that it's ALL mine to receive
Then I'd know I need not question, instead, I simply must believe!

CHAMPION OF GOD

Lord, I don't want to be a prisoner, bound in chains by Hades'
   horde;
Nor overcome by hell's deception as I'm fighting in this war.
I don't want to fear the battle, instead, I ask for strength to fight;
I choose NOT to flee in terror nor run and find a place to hide.
Lord, I want to scale the mountain until I reach the very top;
Climbing upward in my journey with faith and courage not to
   stop.
Increase my ability and gifting to clearly hear Your voice;
And the wisdom to understand, the importance of each choice.
May the weapons of my warfare be all that I will need;
To accomplish Your plan and purpose , to conquer and succeed!
May the powers behind the conflict become weak and lose their
   hold;
As my heart ascends the mountain and my faith leaps forth in
   growth.
Put Your safety net around me , cause my steps to be secure;
As the ledge becomes more narrow and the pathway more
   unsure.
Lord, guide me in this endeavor to scale the mountainside;
Heal the hurtful wounds of battle and increase my ability to fight.
I pray that wisdom from Your Spirit would keep me from a fall;
May I overcome in victory—as a Champion of God!

WALKING DAILY IN HIS LOVE

In the world in which we live, depression takes its hold;
Dealing daily with the negative, leaving nothing left to hope!
But God is such an optimist, He gives hope for each new day;
No matter WHAT the circumstance, His hand will lead the way.
For He is surely faithful and His Word is ALWAYS true;
It will sustain through any storm, and it will help you make it
  through.
Reality is difficult, it crushes hearts of men;
It steals away tomorrow, and leaves an emptiness within.
But endurance to hang on, with a heart to trust in Him;
Will get you through, another day, and give you hope until the
  end.
You see, the Lord will NEVER fail you, when you're standing in
  His Grace;
You are stronger in the long run, and winning in life's race.
There is victory in Jesus—He will ALWAYS be enough;
So, trust Him for the answers, as you are Walking in His Love!

APRIL 30

THE SKIES OF DAWN

I gazed across the morning sky and saw the sunlight's gold;
As dawn revealed creation and all its beauty to behold.
The sky became a canvas beneath the Master's brush
And the grandeur of the moment was created by His touch.
Only for a short time, was I allowed to see
The dawning of the morn and its brilliant majesty.
The birds were live with music as their voices became song;
And for a moment, life was peaceful, across the Skies of Dawn.
It's a time that I could clearly see the Creator's loving hand,
As He painted me a portrait so majestic and so grand!
Yes, today, I looked across the sky as far as I could see
And beheld exquisite colors, displayed especially for me.
I could not help but realize, that this world to HIM belongs;
As I looked across creation and saw the Skies of Dawn!

What Is Faith?
Exceptional Courage
Braveheart
Always More Than Enough
Watchman on the Wall
Army of God
Weapons in the Spirit
You Will Walk with Me
Running Life's Race
Set Apart for Him
Take Time for Every Moment
Love's Compassion
Amazing Love and Grace of God
Solitude of Grace
In a Place Without End
Expression of Joy
In the Cool of the Garden
His Love's Forever Faithful
Faith Without Limits
Will He Come?
Dying Heart
Reaching for Heaven's Throne
Love of His Embrace
Fragrance in the Rose
My Hope Rests in Him
Knowing Him
Wisdom Is God's Treasure
Through Heaven's Pure Eyes
Realm of Love
Covered in His Grace
Arms of God

WHAT IS FAITH?

Faith is belief
Not based upon proof;
It's a lifestyle of living
In the depth of God's truth.
It's embracing HIS favor
To continue the race;
It's walking in blessing—
Standing firm upon faith.
It's facing each battle
And climbing the wall;
It's holding on daily
And trusting in God.
It's FAITH, in the struggle,
That challenges growth;
Releasing courage and boldness—
Filled with TRUE hope!
Yes, faith is belief
Based NOT upon proof;
It's a lifestyle of living,
In the depth of God's Truth!

MAY 2

EXCEPTIONAL COURAGE

Does courage become my attitude, when I'm swept up by the
    storm;
Am I running into battle, holding firm unto the Lord?
You see, my courage is contagious when I take time to follow
    through;
For, as I walk inside HIS Kingdom, I'm being set apart for truth!
So, when I find that I am frail; and sabotaged by fears;
I'll put my trust in Jesus and I'll give Him all my cares.
I'll align myself within His Word, I'll stand steady, strong and
    firm;
Resisting every flame of hell and its fires sent to burn
For I AM a mighty warrior, and I'll stand faithful in my walk;
Rebuking opposition and bowing down before the Rock.
You see, I'm called to be courageous inside the darkest storm;
Finding victory in each battle and strength within the war.
It's the hand of God upon me that will lead me safely through—
It's listening to HIS voice and abiding in HIS truth.
For He IS my only answer, when I'm lost inside the storm;
When the powers of hell are raging, and I'm weary, tired and
    worn.
It's HIS courage that lives within me that revives me once again—
To overcome the turbulence and ride the tempest winds!
Yes, His Spirit gives me victory in the midst of every storm
When I learn to stand in courage and put my trust upon the
    Lord!

MAY 3

BRAVEHEART

I will never lay my sword down nor give up in the fight;
For even in the battle, God STILL controls my life.
You see, He's given me a vision so that I can clearly see;
His every fulfilled promise, in His plans concerning me.
So, I will always follow Jesus and submit to Him, my all;
I won't surrender to defeat, because my faith is strong in God.
I have been given His inheritance, so I will fight until the end
With His light inside my spirit and His love that lives within!
Yes, in Him, I find great courage to stand and fight each day
For even in life's battles, His truth will never sway.
So, I will never lay my sword down nor give up in the fight
I'll be a BRAVEHEART 'til the end, and I will trust HIM, with
    my life!

ALWAYS MORE THAN ENOUGH

To stand in the presence of Glory
Overwhelmed by miraculous love;
To be stirred in my soul and my spirit
And to KNOW, Lord, You're More Than Enough!
To grab hold when I feel I am falling
And keep my heart truly set on the goal;
To arise in the strength of Your calling
And be amazed as my forever unfolds.
To surrender the core of my being—
Every action and motive and thought;
To walk on the path set before me
Giving Glory and Honor to God!
To trust in You as my Savior
With a heart that is daily renewed;
To know that Your hand, Lord, is leading
Every season I'll ever go through.
To let Your peace reign within me
As Your Grace is extended in love;
To know that all You have for me—
Will Always Be MORE Than Enough!

WATCHMAN ON THE WALL

To the Watchman on the Wall, I clarify today
The moving of My Spirit to bring a brand new day.
I've heard your every cry and every prayer that you have prayed;
I've listened so intently to each request that you have made.
You've planted seeds for decades amidst the hard and rocky soil;
Ever faithful, without waver, you have never ceased to toil.
So once again I tell you, take your place upon the wall
Lift your hearts to heaven and watch the mountains fall.
For every seed you've planted will begin to come alive
You'll witness signs and wonders, as they unfold before your eyes.
I have opened heaven's window and breathed LIFE upon the seed
For that which you have sown, you, NOW, will surely reap!
Beware of this new season and stay positioned in your faith
As I bring the dead to life and cause the slumbering to awake.
For the harvest has been seasoned and is about to be revealed;
So, My Child, Behold My Glory—and My Promises Fulfilled!

ARMY OF GOD

By Your Grace we stand at Your Throne—
Such an awesome and Holy place to be;
We give You our hearts in submission
We surrender in service to Thee.
We yield EVERYTHING to Your perfect design,
Your Will and Your Spirit today;
Send a flood of Your River to flow over and cleanse
And wash the assignments of darkness away!
Touch the eyes of our hearts with YOUR eyes to see
Your specific purpose and plan;
Then walk with us daily and show us the way
Anoint us with wisdom to understand.
Give us STRENGTH to be a part of Your army
And YOUR courage to stand and fight;
Disperse Your ministering angels from heaven
To pursue and set demons to flight.
Make us a part of Your Army, Oh God
Give us ears to hear Your call;
Direct EVERY step our feet will walk
Help us, Lord, to NOT stumble and fall.
Lord, raise up an army for this end-time war
Reveal YOUR strategy from above;
Give us insight in the midst of it all—
Pour out Your Mercy, Your Grace and Your Love.
And when the battle is finally over
And every saint of God is called home;
May YOUR praises of glory and honor be heard
FOREVER around heaven's throne!

MAY 7

WEAPONS IN THE SPIRIT

We wrestle NOT against flesh and blood, but powers of the air;
For Satan and his forces, are prowling everywhere!
So, the weapons of our warfare, are neither made of what we SEE;
Rather Weapons in the Spirit, designed to give us VICTORY!
They are weapons that demolish, every stronghold we will face;
They are Weapons in God's Spirit, they are strong and will not
    break!
The precious NAME OF JESUS, and GOD'S WORD within our
    heart;
Are mighty weapons we possess, to tear the devil's schemes apart!
Also, the obedience to FAST and our PRAISE from deep within;
Are weapons we must use, in overcoming him!
We dare not forget the BLOOD, that was shed so long ago;
For it holds such strength and power, to defeat the darkest foe!
Then, there's the weapon of AGREEMENT, which carries power
    to the throne;
It breaks through every barrier, and every power known!
And finally there is PRAYER, flowing from the depths within;
To connect us to a Living God, and blessings without end!
So, the weapons that we fight with, are not weapons that we SEE;
Instead, they're Weapons in the Spirit, designed to give us
    VICTORY!

YOU WILL WALK WITH ME

Father, even at my weakest point, I KNOW that You are there;
Even when I feel bombarded by the voices of despair.
Even when my road grows weary, and I can't face another day;
When the pain is overwhelming, and there are no words to say.
I still know that You are with me—I don't know HOW, Lord, I
    just do;
And I know I'd never make it, if You weren't there to see me
    through.
So, I thank You for Your comfort and the peace I feel within;
I praise You for that deep-down strength, that only YOU, can
    give!
And as I face this coming season, I will NOT be afraid,
Nor relinquish precious moments where I can stand on FAITH!
I will trust You, in this time of life, knowing You will surely SEE;
Everything that I have need of and ALL concerning me!

MAY 9

RUNNING LIFE'S RACE

The race was growing weary and I stumbled to my knees;
It's like I could not go another mile nor even stand upon my feet.
My vision had been clouded and I could no longer see the finish;
The focus of my heart was strained and my strength had been
    diminished.
The explosive vigor I once had to run the race until the end;
Had quickly vanished into nothing as piercing anguish had set in.
I knew not what to do so I sat in deep despair;
And then I felt a gentle hand brush softly through my hair.
I looked up to see my Jesus, kneeling at my side;
His loving words of comfort seemed to fill me up inside.
We just sat there for a while and I rested in His love;
You see, He knew that I had fallen and was unable to get up.
He waited, oh, so patiently within His love and grace;
He wiped every single teardrop that formed upon my face.
It's as if He knew my every struggle and all my inner pain;
He KNEW that I was weary and that I felt completely drained.
But He showed me, in the race, HIS will, was being done;
For I HAD to face each obstacle so I could learn to overcome.
He assured me of His presence even when I failed to see
That He was right there all the time, running side by side with
    me.
Yes, the race sometimes seems weary but there IS a finish line;
And I will never run alone for He is ALWAYS by my side.
My heart was strengthened in an instant from His loving warm
    embrace;
He then helped me to my feet and put me BACK into the race.
Now I'm running once again the race I'm called to run;
Secure that He'll be with me until my life on earth is done!

Therefore we also, since we are surrounded by so great a cloud of witnesses, let us lay aside every weight, and the sin which so easily ensnares us, and let us run with endurance the race that is set before us.

—HEBREWS 12:1, NKJV

MAY 10

SET APART FOR HIM

There's a chamber in my heart
That has been expanded to receive;
Revelation from the throne room
And ALL God has for me.
My ears are being trained
To HEAR the voice of God;
To understand His mysteries
And walk where angels walk.
God is pouring forth His wisdom
And imparting revelation deep within;
Giving knowledge that FAR surpasses
My human ability to comprehend.
He has extended the realm of heaven
And touched my ears to HEAR;
He has pierced through utter chaos
And made EVERYTHING so clear.
He has given me direction
With a purpose and a plan;
My life was set in motion
At the sound of His command.
His angels go before me
His Holy Spirit lives within;
He has HIS mark upon me
To be one—Set Apart for Him!

May 11

Take Time for Every Moment

Make each and every moment count, for tomorrow may NOT
   come;
Take time to smell the roses, don't leave anything undone.
For, each and every moment, has significant appeal
Here—then gone FOREVER—but it NEVER just stands still!
Those seemingly important things, will tend to steal away;
The importance of EACH moment, in the life you live each day.
So, take time to stop and ponder, the beauty of God's Love;
Take time to spot HIS handiwork, and His blessings from above.
And when you do, you'll see, things you NEVER saw before;
Like the value of relationships—which bring life's TRUE rewards!
Grasp and hold each moment, and take the time to see;
The importance of ALL things, in their true simplicity!
Take Time for Every Moment, and life WILL come alive,
Your heart will be refreshed, and your faith will be revived!

MAY 12

LOVE'S COMPASSION

Beneath the starry skies at night in a place where I'm alone
My mind can't help but wander and my heart just seems to roam.
For it's in the night I'm swallowed by the darkness that surrounds
And it's hard to reach for hope when my life's so broken down.
You see, I'm lost inside the shadows and no one seems to care
I look around for help but there is no one there.
So I cry to God for answers and ask for light to enter in
For peace to fill my heart and give me hope to live again.
It's then I understand, I've never truly been alone
For God's Spirit's my companion—inside me is His home!
Yes, this journey has been long but I now see the light of day
He was with me all the time, even when I'd lost my way.
He came with Love's Compassion and rescued me from harm
He heard my cry from heaven and opened up His arms.
Like a shepherd He now leads me through the pastures lush and
    green
Where He feeds me at His table and meets my every need.

Amazing Love and Grace of God

I once allowed such pointless noise
To live within my soul;
And then I heard the Spirit's voice
And felt His soft wind blow.
He gently spoke the words, "Be Still"
And my heart filled with His peace;
My storms had finally faced the calm—
And the tides of turmoil ceased.
He counseled me to lay aside
The life that I HAD lived;
And devote myself completely
To a life ALIVE in Him!
He filled me with His Spirit—
He redeemed and set me free;
He delivered me from certain death
And calmed the raging sea.
He hushed each lie of condemnation—
And poured His mercy from the throne;
When I gave my heart to Jesus
And my life to Him alone.
Even NOW it's so incredible
I cannot help but stand in awe;
You see, today, I'm STILL amazed—
At the Awesome Love AND Grace of God!

MAY 14

SOLITUDE OF GRACE

Underneath Your canopy,
In the shadow of Your wings;
My heart seeks peaceful refuge,
And the solace Your love brings.
Deep within the crevasse
And Your Solitude of Grace;
Where the voice of condemnation
Cannot have a resting place.
Where hopes and dreams are possible
In the presence of Your love;
And hope cannot be shattered,
Nor yield to the corrupt.
Lord, I have a desperate need
To live within YOUR Hiding Place;
Beneath the shadow of Your wings,
Within YOUR Solitude of Grace.

In a Place Without End

When spring flowers bloom and birds sing their songs;
When, GENTLE, are hearts—and rejected, belong!
When grace from above, falls like the dew;
When peace fills the air, and HOPE is renewed.
When the sun never sets and the tears are all dried;
When unspeakable joy, set all heartache aside.
When praise is the fragrance, that rides on the breeze,
When sounds of rejoicing, dance atop trees!
When a whisper from God, breaks through the night;
When one glance from HIS heart, makes EVERYTHING right.
When love becomes passion, and thanksgiving a hymn;
When ALL Things Are Well—in a Place Without End!

MAY 16

EXPRESSION OF JOY

To be Your Expression of Joy
And to let it indeed be my strength;
To worship from my innermost being
As deep calls out unto deep.
Your anointing, Lord, overcomes darkness
Through the power of your released love;
Your joy becomes my expression
That ALWAYS, is more than enough.
Yes, I am Your Expression of Joy
So that all the world may know;
That You are among Your people
And goodness is sure to unfold.
So, even in perilous times
When trials try so hard to subdue;
My heart will continue to PRAISE
And my joy will be found in YOU!
For, I am Your Expression of Joy
And, You, Lord, are indeed my strength;
I will worship from my innermost being
Allowing deep to call unto deep!

MAY 17

IN THE COOL OF THE GARDEN

To walk with You daily, is where YOU'VE set my feet—
And in the Cool of the Garden is where our hearts meet.
Lord, this is the place, where I hear Your voice;
Where I'm lost in Your presence and overcome with love's joy.
Yes, in the Cool of the Garden, You have opened my eyes;
And revealed Heaven's Glory and called me to rise.
You have poured forth Your Spirit and allowed me to see;
The depth of Your love, sincerely lavished on me.
So, in the Cool of the Garden, I will seek You by faith;
I will walk with You, Lord, and find rest in Your shade.
For, it's only in You, my heart knows true peace;
As You shine forth Your light and direct my two feet.
So, Lord, Help me to follow and seek You EACH day;
In the Cool of the Garden, Where Love NEVER Fades!

MAY 18

HIS LOVE'S FOREVER FAITHFUL

(Read Psalm 13)

When I'm feeling overwhelmed
Fear comes to paralyze;
It tries to rob my peace
And put a veil upon my eyes.
Doubt THEN seeks a home
Like a leech upon my heart;
It comes to steal my faith away
And catch my mind off guard.
BUT I know that this is NOT of God
So I activate my faith;
I align myself in Jesus
And trust His loving grace!
For I cannot let fear hold me
In a grip that overwhelms;
Nor let self-pity enter
To come and hold me down.
So, instead I make a choice
To get myself in gear;
Rising up in power
Waging WAR against my fears!
Finding hope in Jesus
And trusting in His grace;
No longer overwhelmed
Instead, now LOST in His embrace.
Yes, I find God's Grace Sufficient
To come and meet my every need;
You see, His Love's Forever Faithful
And He Is Always Watching Me!

FAITH WITHOUT LIMITS

When my dreams and visions seem to die
And my expectations limit God;
His Spirit stirs my faith within
With a hope to carry on.
You see, Jesus comes to raise the dead,
He speaks LIFE to dying seed;
For, it's the power of HIS Spirit
That awakens hearts, and sets men free.
Life so often seems to crumble
But He's faithful deep within;
For, with Jesus, EVERYTHING is possible—
There's not a thing that's kept from Him.
There is nothing Christ cannot undo—
When seeds of faith are stirred to see;
That my God, can do ANYTHING—
When I CHOOSE to just believe!

WILL HE COME?

When hope has lost its meaning and I've nothing left inside;
When I can't find rhyme nor reason, to the pain that plaques my
   mind,
When my very soul's been captured and I'm a prisoner to my
   SELF;
Will God reach through the chasm and offer me His help?
When the sun has stopped its shining and the winds are harsh to
   blow;
Will heaven's window open, or will it, just stay closed?
When reality is shattered and I'm busted, tired and weak;
Will the well I've dug, be deep enough, to draw forth inner
   strength?
Will I find that in this season, where the fire burns so hot;
I can trust HIM for the answers and behold the hand of God.
Will I see His very finger, reach down inside my soul;
To stir the fiery embers—creating diamonds out of coal?
Will He come inside the chaos and calm my silent screams;
Will He comfort pain's illusion and restore my broken dreams?
Will hope become the beacon, that watches o'er my night
Even when I cannot function, and I have NO strength to fight?
Will God be there to see me through, in the midst of where I am,
When I'm on a downward spiral—will He extend His
   outstretched hand?
Will He find that I'm worth saving and breathe His breath of life
   in me,
Will He keep me 'til tomorrow—delivered from the enemy?
YES, I KNOW, He'll raise His voice and command the winds to
   cease;
In the midst of where I am—HE WILL COME—AND Breathe
   HIS Peace!

MAY 21

DYING HEART

Sometimes a heart can die, but continues, still, to beat;
As a life goes through the motions, crumbled by defeat.
Not a single soul may notice, another's heart that's died;
Nor the emptiness and pain, that's buried deep inside.
But, Jesus SEES the emptiness, and the bruise of every pain;
He knows each bitter sorrow and every heartache that remains.
He's well aware of uncried tears, and hidden hurts within;
He wants to heal the injured heart and give back life, again!
But a heart can ONLY trust, that Jesus KNOWS what's best;
To believe His Word WILL stand, through every trial and test!
Yes, He's aware of every teardrop, that falls upon the ground ;
And He's there, inside the heartache, to turn ALL things around!
He opens heaven's window and He pours forth loving Grace;
To the Dying Heart, in need of—a precious touch of His embrace!

REACHING FOR HEAVEN'S THRONE

In the midst of tribulation and chaos in my life;
I often search for answers that will readily shed light.
But sometimes there are seasons that tend to be so dark;
Where struggles become problems and leave a plague upon my
    heart.
I cry out, "Abba Father, Come and Rescue Me";
And then I wait, inside the shadows, for the enemy to flee.
And then comes revelation deep within my soul;
That no matter, WHAT, I go through—My God's STILL, in
    control!
You see, He often brings the season that will show me what's
    inside;
So that He can cleanse my heart, and I no longer have to hide.
He allows the sin to surface that I never knew was there;
Then He restores to me, my purpose, and frees me from the
    snare.
He has called me unto righteousness, so, in me, He will fulfill;
All that will be needed, to cleanse, restore, and heal.
So, when I find myself—in a season that's unknown;
May I cry out, "Abba Father," and Reach for Heaven's Throne!

LOVE OF HIS EMBRACE

God's Love pulls back the curtain
And revelation fills my soul;
My heart becomes a compass
For HIS loving hands to hold.
He guides me through the night
And gives me rest in Him;
He fills me with HIS peace
And overwhelming love within.
His Spirit gives me courage
And a passion to pursue;
His Kingdom Life on Earth
By all I say and do.
I find that I am captured
By my Savior's loving grace;
My heart has found its home
Within the love of His embrace!

FRAGRANCE IN THE ROSE

God touched the beauty of the rose
And gave it color from above;
He merely brushed the tiny petals,
And caused the bud to open up.
He held it close to His own heart
So very early in the morn;
And then He put it in His garden,
And placed upon it—thorns!
If the eye will look more closely
It becomes aware to see;
That the thorns upon the stem
ONLY make the rose complete.
You see, there's nothing quite as lovely
To stir a heart to look above;
Than the grandeur of this flower
That started as a tiny bud.
God, in tender passion,
Revealed HIS beauty to behold;
Then Jesus blew HIS breath upon it,
And placed the Fragrance in the Rose!

MY HOPE RESTS IN HIM

When heaven comes down
And touches the earth;
My heart is stirred within;
For His Glory's My Crown,
And He is my worth;
And ALL of My Hope
Rests in Him!

KNOWING HIM

As I sit here in the silence, listening to the rustling breeze;
I can hear the lovely songbird, as my Jesus sings to me.
I can breathe in every promise through every breath I take;
And be lost inside His presence, and wrapped in His embrace.
Yes, I'm growing close to Jesus, because I'm abiding in His love;
I'm bathed with heaven's peace, flowing from the throne above.
It's at this very moment, in the stillness of it all;
That I can see with clearer vision, the very handprint of my God.
It's like all I'll ever be, is what I let HIM be within;
You see, His purpose in MY life, has ALWAYS been in Knowing
    HIM!

MAY 27

Wisdom Is God's Treasure

Wisdom's the result from
Spending time with God;
Being led by His own Spirit
And walking where HE walks.
It's admitting in my heart
That I know not everything;
It's seeking counsel daily
And then humbly listening.
It's taking proper time
To pray before I speak;
It's waiting on the Lord
For every answer that I seek.
It is rejoicing in the WAIT
Not fretting in it all;
It's positioning my spirit
To HEAR the voice of God.
It's receiving ALL He has
With boldness deep within;
It's stepping out in faith
With no regard of where I've been.
Wisdom's walking in obedience
With HIS courage in my heart;
Knowing His direction will protect—
And His understanding will stand guard.
Yes, only God gives me TRUE wisdom
When I search for it as gold;
For Godly Wisdom Is a Treasure
That can only come from Heaven's Throne.

MAY 28

THROUGH HEAVEN'S PURE EYES

Lord, when You look at me—what do You see;
Am I becoming the person—You planned me to be?
Am I following the pathway, that's narrow and straight;
Do I ask Your direction and then patiently wait?
Do I listen for answers, that will point out YOUR way;
Can I be trusted to hear You, and ALL You will say?
Does my heart hold the answers, and do You hold the key;
Will YOU unlock all the secrets—and show them to me?
Will I ever be able to see what YOU see;
Am I becoming the person—You planned me to be?
Will I ever see ME, through Heaven's Pure Eyes;
If You lifted the veil, would my heart be surprised?
Oh, God, in my wonder, I am truly amazed—
Of Your greatness and honor, and Your loving ways!

MAY 29

REALM OF LOVE

In the stillness of the moment I find myself aware;
That I am standing in Your presence and consumed within Your
  care.
I can feel Your heart touch mine with the fragrance of the dew;
And I'm compelled to be drawn closer until I'm completely found
  in You!
It's in that place of Glory where the Holy Spirit dwells;
That I find myself at peace, inside that realm where love prevails.
And in that very moment as my heart gives way to You;
I'm convinced there's nothing greater that my life could dare
  pursue.
So, know that I will seek You with all my heart and soul;
For it's only, Lord, in You, that my life is truly whole.

MAY 30

COVERED IN HIS GRACE

If not for God's Grace, I could not stand,
Amidst the seas of life;
I could not dare to face the day,
Without the LOVE of Christ!
It's, He, who leads me as I walk,
It's, He, who shows the way;
He gives me strength to overcome,
And make it through each day!
And even when I'm lonely,
I. still. am NOT alone;
For, HE, is always with me,
To lift each heavy load!
And, though, I may not understand
The struggles that I face;
I know I'll ALWAYS make it,
Because, I'm Covered in His Grace!

Arms of God

God's precious loving grace, will see me through my worst;
When I learn to trust in Him, and ALWAYS put Him FIRST!
Hope's consistent to prevail, when I look unto the Lord;
I've found that perseverance brings, the richness of reward!
For light is promised in the darkness, in the times I cannot see;
It's then, my God is guiding and truly leading me!
So, when I cannot understand—I'll trust that Jesus knows it ALL;
I'll stand firm within my faith, sheltered by the Arms of God!

JUNE

Gentle Breeze

Maintaining Balance

Led by His Spirit

Heaven Is Breaking Through

The Wind of the Spirit Is Blowing

His Love Will Always Be Your Guide

God's Greatest Treasures

Reaping His Reward

For Such a Time As This

Pathway of a Pilgrim

It's He Who's in Control

Loosed from Captivity

Glory's Flow

He's the Promise I Seek

Joy in the Struggle

Day of New Beginning

Summoned to Glory

Mountaintop Reflections

The Host of Heaven

Holy Realm of Worship

His Healing Power

Vision for My Future

Path of Life

Little Acts of Kindness

Finding Peace in Jesus

Walking in Blessing

Contentment for Today

Following Footsteps

His Tender Sweet Compassion

Arms of Grace

JUNE 1

GENTLE BREEZE

There's a Gentle Breeze a blowin'
Across the wayward mile;
Atop the mountains majesty—
Where angelic beauty smiles.
Could it be the breath of God
Breathing down on me;
Is His Spirit simply wooing
In this mystic mystery?
A wave of heaven's hand
Creates a story within me;
And I become a timeless treasure—
For all the world to see!
Yes, precious are His children
Clothed in love's display;
The eloquence of heaven
Birthed to show the way.
Could it be that when He breathes
I'm alive within the Son;
And the fragrance of His breath
Becomes the LIFE within my lungs?
Yes, His breath becomes the wind
Inside the Gentle Breeze;
He raptures my heart upward—
And sets THIS captive free!

JUNE 2

MAINTAINING BALANCE

Lord, may I maintain my balance—through all my highs AND
    lows
Sustained with grace from heaven and my faith in You, alone.
May my afflictions last a moment and then quickly dull and fade;
As the breath from Your own nostrils, comes to blow them all
    away.
May I find Your very favor in the midst of every trial
And receive, YOUR joy promised, to walk another mile.
In my prison, keep me singing even when there's nothing left;
Lord, may my eyes be ever upward and NEVER upon self.
And then when HIGH times come, may I never soon forget
Your benefits extended, through the blowing of Your breath.
Like the dewdrops kiss the flowers, place Your loving seal on me;
And sustain me in the circumstance, no matter what I SEE.
Lord, Your faithfulness is with me, in my highs and in my lows:
Yes, I find You're always with me—I will NEVER walk alone.
So, I thank You for Your grace and all that You bestow
Whether on the mountaintop or in the valley low!
For, it's only in these seasons that my heart will truly know
Your love and grace extended—throughout the process of my
    growth!

JUNE 3

LED BY HIS SPIRIT

As long as you stay where you are—
Then you must know, THAT'S where you'll be;
If you stumble along in the darkness,
Then understand, THAT'S all you'll see!
You can choose to have your heart's view clouded
Or you can climb OUT of the miry clay;
You can wallow in darkness and pity
Or you can yield to His leading today.
For, it's only when YOU make a choice
To finally stand up and fight;
That your heart will witness His Glory
And YOU will be led by His light.
He graciously offers the answers
And provides you a way of escape;
He sends forth His Sweet Holy Spirit
And makes all of your crooked ways straight.
He opens the gates into Glory
He extends forth His righteous right hand;
He pursues you with His Holy Passion
And endows you with new strength to stand.
HE is the Light in Your Darkness
Yes, HE, is the Truth and the Way;
Behold, now, HIS Glory before you
And Be Led By His Spirit Today!

JUNE 4

HEAVEN IS BREAKING THROUGH

There's a holy invasion where God's gates open wide
And heaven breaks through, with a bright shining light.
Yes, eternity pierces the natural realm
And invades the world's darkness with God at its helm.
It's shaking the shackles that bind hearts of men
Breathing Spirit-Filled Life, where death had once been.
It's loosing the hold and setting men free
Releasing EACH heart, into their own destiny.
It's God's Spirit made full—it's what's at the core;
It's His "breaker anointing" being called forth.
It's a holy invasion where heaven breaks through
And the Spirit of God comes to seek and pursue.
It's the kingdom that's promised to those who receive—
And it comes to the heart that is open to see.
It's the Spirit of God falling fresh upon men
Bringing eternal glory and life without end.

The Wind of the Spirit Is Blowing

Released is the Wind of the Spirit
Which rides on the breath of God's breeze;
It restores, it heals, it renews—
Its anointing brings men to their knees.
It's God's love so lavishly showered
Upon the Wind of the Spirit that blows;
Touching hearts filled with passion for Jesus
Reaching down to the depth of one's soul.
It's God's breath upon those that are seeking
As His glory from heaven descends;
It's the gift of His own precious Spirit
Released in POWER and sent forth to men.
Receive in your hearts, saints of God,
What He is doing afresh and anew;
His anointing is being sent forth—
Let His Spirit breath NEW life in you—
For the Wind of the Spirit IS Blowing
Do not miss what God has for this hour;
Open your heart to His Spirit—
Be filled with HIS strength and HIS power!
For He's breathing His breath now from heaven
He is sending His latter rain;
Reach up, Saints of God, and touch Glory
TODAY—Be Forever Changed!

JUNE 6

HIS LOVE WILL ALWAYS BE YOUR GUIDE

The Savior yearns so desperately for you to have fellowship with
  Him;
To receive His grace within your life—and to know, His desire to
  call you, friend!
You see, He's called you to this very place—my friend, for such a
  time as this;
You'll find your life will change forever, when your heart is drawn
  to His.
It's His tender love that's wooing you, He has called you for His
  own;
He desires your full attention, to be focused on Him, alone.
Seek Him while He can be found, let Him touch your heart today;
Turn your eyes upon the Savior, let Him come and have His way.
Let your spirit man be opened and receive the gift He gives;
Which is the presence of His Spirit, who comes to draw you close
  to Him!
There's such tender loving fellowship, when you're walking side
  by side;
He'll never leave you nor forsake you—His Love Will Always Be
  Your Guide!

GOD'S GREATEST TREASURES

He made the mountains and the deserts, the forest and the trees;
Yet, still His GREATEST treasures, are the lives of you and me.
He put the color in the sunset and placed it in the sky;
It's like He opened glory's portal just for you and I.
He sprinkled earth's sweet landscape with the moisture of the
    dew
He gave the birds a song to sing just for me and you.
He made the heavens and the earth, the oceans and the seas;
But when He looks for pleasure, He always looks to you and me.
It's like He has a treasure chest—full of jewels and gems;
And He holds each of them with value and loves every one of
    them.
Their colors are magnificent, such brilliant lovely hues;
For that which He holds close are the lives of me and you.
Yes, we're God's Greatest Treasures, we hold the glory of His
    Light
We're the gemstones of His heart and we're the apple of His eye!

JUNE 8

REAPING HIS REWARD

My heart does not fear
For it's turned to the Lord;
I don't focus on worry
Instead, HIS just reward.
You see, God is my hope
He's my beacon in life;
He's the strength in my heart
He's my bright shining light.
Yes, God is the place
Where I safely dwell;
HIS habitation is mine
It's where His love does prevail.
I am hidden away
Where the Lord reigns supreme;
Where the beauty of God
Is all that is seen.
So I'll lift up my head
In the glory of praise;
And I'll walk where God walks
In a realm unashamed.
For my heart has been set
Upon God's lovely face;
It's His power of love
That is MY saving grace.
Yes, He holds my future
So I'll wait on the Lord;
I'll find MY strength in Him
And I'll Reap HIS Reward.

JUNE 9

FOR SUCH A TIME AS THIS

I know I've been created
For Such a Time As This;
For I can feel God's Holy Spirit
Pouring forth great confidence.
His passion stirs within me
And brings me to my knees;
I am seeing MORE of Him
And looking less and less at me.
The favor of the Lord
Has found a home within;
I'm drawn into His presence
Where my heart does worship Him.
His anointing is my covering
It's His lovely fruit bestowed;
It's the fragrance of the Father
Flowing freely from the Throne.
It's God's Precious Holy Spirit
Releasing ministry through me;
That will touch a wounded nation—
Heal and set the captives free.
Yes, for Such a Time As This
My life's released to be;
A vessel for God's Kingdom
And His light for all to see!

June 10

Pathway of a Pilgrim

I may be just a pilgrim, traveling through a foreign land;
But I know where I am headed and I'm following God's plan.
You see, I could never face tomorrow in this place I don't belong;
If His hand weren't there to guide me, and I knew not right from
    wrong.
I depend upon His loving care and His strategic battle plan;
To help me walk a daily walk, within this foreign land.
Yes, I may be just a pilgrim, in this place I'm passing through;
But there is joy in the journey, just knowing WHERE I'm headed
    to!
You see, the Pathway of a Pilgrim is a road that leads toward
    HOME—
And the place I find myself, TODAY—is just a stepping stone!

It's He Who's in Control

In the midst of worldly chaos, God's Spirit spoke to me;
He moved with power upon my heart—cast out fear and set me
 free.
You see, His ways are not my ways, there's no reason to His
 rhyme;
I may THINK He's running late, when in fact, He's right on time.
So, often He will call me, as His vessel to the throne;
To trust and wait upon Him—to put my faith in HIM, alone!
And in that time, I find myself, in intercession more and more;
Waiting patiently for HIS Will, for the battle IS the Lord's!
So, I relinquish all my worldly rights, and MY agenda to
 complain;
I turn my heart upon the Savior, and HIS victory I proclaim!
You see, my EYES may see confusion but my HEART is safe
 within His hands;
For no matter WHAT the circumstance, I GUARANTEE—God
 Has a Plan!
When I feel I'm in the balance, and need to know which way to
 go;
I will draw in close to God's heart—for It Is HE Who's in Control.

JUNE 12

LOOSED FROM CAPTIVITY

It was not 'til I was broken, God could come and set me free;
Releasing HIS abundance, to be all that I could be.
He placed within my heart, an awesome joy to behold;
And then He wrapped me in His Glory, within the covering of
    His robe.
He gave balance to my feet, upon the battlefield;
He opened up my heart, and humbly taught me how to yield.
He led me forth from darkness to abundant life in Him;
He breathed His breath upon me and set me free from sin.
He removed my limitations and gave me wings to fly;
He empowered me for greatness and thrust me to the sky.
Yes, I hold on to ALL His promises, and the love He has
    bestowed;
He Has Loosed Me from Captivity, set me free and made me
    whole!

June 13

Glory's Flow

The weight of many waters, pour forth from Heaven's Throne;
And those beneath the portal, find themselves in Glory's Flow.
They smell God's fragrant breath, upon the rushing wind;
As it covers like a blanket, and stirs their hearts within.
They hear the mighty rumble upon the distant shore;
They are listening to His voice, and asking Him for MORE!
In a mighty move of God, His anointing's flowing through;
He is pouring out His blessings, upon the kiss of morning dew.
Yes, the weight of many waters, are coming from His Throne;
And those beneath the portal, find themselves in Glory's Flow!

JUNE 14

HE'S THE PROMISE I SEEK

The Lord searches my heart
He knows each thought that I think;
He knows when I'm awake
And He knows when I sleep.
My journey's description
Is the path HE lays forth;
It's the road that I follow
In pursuit of the Lord.
It's the promise of God
My heart seeks to fulfill;
To become MORE like Him—
To let Christ be revealed.
May HIS image be found
In the depth of my soul;
May the wealth of God's Son
Be the treasure I hold.
For it's only in Jesus
That I'm truly complete;
He's the Way, Truth and Life—
He's the Promise I Seek!

JUNE 15

JOY IN THE STRUGGLE

May you find Joy in the Struggle—and KNOW, God is enough;
May you find peace within the trial, when you FEEL like giving
    up.
For, you're not immune from problems, but God will always
    guide you through;
He will open doors OR shut them, He'll do what's BEST for you!
And even in affliction or the bitter sting of pain;
Remember, nothing from the Lord will ever be in vain!
So, trust the Lord for answers, in your struggles day to day,
Just know that He is with you and He will guide you on life's way!

JUNE 16

DAY OF NEW BEGINNING

God's love never changes,
It forever lives within;
His Grace never fails,
Nor will it ever end.
He always blows His breath
Upon the ones He loves;
He touches hearts that hurt
And His answers are enough!
There is nothing in the world
Like the presence of the Lord;
Even in the midst of trials
And tribulations that come forth.
It's a Day of New Beginning,
Where His rays of light peek through;
Where His Grace is ALL sufficient,
And ALL things are made new!

JUNE 17

SUMMONED TO GLORY

He put a crown upon my head
And led me through an open door;
Into the chamber of His throne room—
And THEN His anointing He outpoured.
It was like a light from heaven
Beaming through all time and space;
Sent to summon me for glory
To stand before Him—Face to Face!
The words He spoke were awesome
Yet not a single sound was heard;
For in the presence of His greatness
Only angels seemed to stir.
I found myself before Him
Lying prostrate on the floor;
For I could no longer stand
In the presence of the Lord.
He caressed my heart so tenderly
And stirred love's passion deep within;
His very presence seemed to wash me—
I had NEVER felt so cleansed.
He touched my life and changed me
Set me free from sin and shame;
I was in the presence of His Glory
And I would NEVER be the same.
He's now captured me FOREVER
He has filled me to the brim;
My cup is truly overflowing
With the love I feel for Him.
I was Summoned to His Glory—
Into the very presence of the Lord;
To partake of ALL His riches
And His fullness of reward!

JUNE 18
MOUNTAINTOP REFLECTIONS

Lord, I'm so tired of the struggles, and fatigue within the storm;
It seems the overwhelming battles, just continue on and on!
I need a Mountaintop Reflection—a place where I am not afraid;
To look upon the valley, and the progress I have made.
When I'm walking the valley, I know EVERYTHING I face;
Will bring me to my knees, and Your protected warm embrace!
I know, I NEED the valley, and every struggle that it brings;
So I can learn to overcome, with triumphant victories
I know it's meant for GOOD, so help me understand;
That even in the valley, I'm STILL in Your perfect plan.
Because, often it is hard to SEE, when standing IN the storm;
When I FEEL so battle weary, broken, tired and worn!
I need a Mountaintop Reflection, encouraging me to gaze upon;
The victories in the valley, and each success within the storm!

THE HOST OF HEAVEN

There comes a wave of harvest
Released upon the land;
A provoking in the Spirit
That moves by God's command.
There's a passing of the mantle
With fresh anointing for this day;
The unsealed being opened
To illuminate the way.
The Son of man sends angels
To gather in our midst;
They lead us into harvest
And into righteousness.
To achieve the spoken promise,
All WE know, must end;
So that God can do it through us
As all the Glory goes to Him.
There's a hope of each our calling
To awaken every seed;
That goes beyond the promise
To all that will receive.

JUNE 20

HOLY REALM OF WORSHIP

I've been blessed to dream in brilliant colors, and to touch God's
lovely face;
To dance in heaven's throne room, and feel the warmth of His
embrace.
I've heard sweet secrets whispered softly, of His mysteries yet to
come;
I've been lost within His presence and immersed within His Love.
I've been entrusted in His Spirit to go beyond ALL that I know;
To the inner courts of heaven, to the footstool of the throne.
I've seen His Holy Realm of Glory, I have worshiped at His feet;
I have laid my burdens down and been filled up, with His peace.
I have smelled the sweet aroma and the fragrance of the Lord;
I've been overcome with passion and found my face upon the
floor.
Yes, I've been to Heaven's Throne Room, in the Presence of the
King—
In the Holy Realm of Worship, Where HIS Glory Reigns
Supreme!

JUNE 21

HIS HEALING POWER

Heal me, Oh Lord, and I shall be healed;
Send me Your Spirit and I shall be filled!
Take hold of my hand, Lord—You lead me through;
Draw my heart closer, that I might see You!
I cry out to You, in my depth of distress;
And I ask for Your Will—nothing more, nothing less!
Lord, Your Word gives life, Your truth sets me free;
It's Your hand that guides—it's Your Spirit that leads.
You, Lord, deliver, from the darkness of night;
Into Your Holy presence and Your marvelous light.
So, in You, I believe, and my confidence soars;
For, in YOU, nothing's too hard OR impossible, Lord!
I shall not die but live and declare
My eyes will look up as I lift up my prayer.
You are Alpha and Omega and You dwell within;
You are my answer—You're the beginning and end!
So, I will believe even when I can't see;
Knowing every prayer has been heard and every tear has
    been seen!
As I call, Lord, please answer, and take hold of my hand;
For everything I go through, is merely PART of Your Plan!

JUNE 22

VISION FOR MY FUTURE

Without Vision for My Future, it's awfully hard to SEE;
All that lies ahead, in what You have planned for me.
Without perception in my heart, it's hard to comprehend;
What I know to be as TRUTH—and what You've planted deep
within.
For, I know that I am MORE, than a conqueror through You;
But, when I rely upon my FEELINGS, I often miss out on what's
TRUE!
Lord, I can't be ruled by feelings, or thoughts that come my way;
I must rest assured in KNOWING, that worldly cares WILL fade
away.
I must learn to look away, from all that will distract;
With Vision for My Future, looking FORWARD and not back!
Lord, encourage me with hope, and direction for today;
Give me Vision, for My Future—with Your Light to Guide the
Way!

PATH OF LIFE

There are no such things as accidents, when you're living for the
King;
NOTHING is by happenstance—He's in control of
EVERYTHING!
Yes, you may often wonder, why things happen as they do;
But, God's in charge of everything, that has to do with YOU!
He prepares the path before you, then He walks right by your
side;
He's your partner on this Path of Life—He leads, directs, and
guides!
The will of God does far outweigh, coincidence for you;
And He has His own good reasons, why things happen as they
do.
So, you need not be afraid, because HE has a perfect plan;
Just stay upon the Path of Life, knowing, HE, has got your hand!

JUNE 24

LITTLE ACTS OF KINDNESS

It's the Little Acts of Kindness, that so greatly touch our lives;
Those little unexpected things, that take us by surprise!
It's the heartfelt love of caring, with humility to share;
And the tender way of showing, that God is ALWAYS there!
It's the Little Acts of Kindness, that seem to mean the most;
In the middle of the crisis, where there seems to be no hope.
It's those Little Acts of Kindness, that won't be soon forgot;
Because the sacrifice IS noticed, and captured deep in thought!
You see, the Father seeks to find, true humility within;
And He watches acts of kindness—that point another's heart to
    Him!

June 25

Finding Peace in Jesus

In the cool of the day
beneath the shade of the trees;
My heart ponders the Lord
as I fall to my knees.
The wind softly whispers
His voice in my ear;
And I'm drawn to His presence
by all that I hear.
And then in the breeze,
His fragrance drifts to my nose;
It's like the breath of the dawn
being sent through the rose.
The beauty before me
has captured my eyes—
To behold Him in glory
is my ultimate prize.
For it's when my heart seeks Him
that I truly find
The touch of His Spirit
that reaches through time.
It's then that I'm certain
He lives within me;
For I have tasted His goodness
and I know that it's sweet.
So I come to this place
beneath the shade of the trees
To spend time in His presence
and find rest in His peace!

WALKING IN BLESSING

My destiny's accomplished,
My destination's reached;
Now I'm Walking in Blessing
I'm receiving Increase!
I have peace in my heart
I possess God's resource;
I have more than enough
Because of the Lord.
My life's in His hands
In Him I'm secure;
I will never have lack
I will never be poor.
For I'm Walking in Blessing
I'm receiving Increase;
I am loved by my Father
And I am filled with His peace.
You see, my Father is wealthy
He owns it ALL;
So I am Walking in Blessing—
GLORY TO GOD!

Contentment for Today

Teach me, Lord, to understand, each thing You bring my way;
Whether blessing, joy, and happiness, or the sorrow of heartache.
Help me not grow weary, when I feel life's bitter sting;
May I run life's race with vigor, no matter WHAT it brings!
May my spirit soar beyond, each circumstance I face;
To a place of peaceful refuge, within Your arms of Grace!
Help me, Lord, to be content at the door where heartache knocks
Give me strength to carry on, and the courage not to stop.
I pray, my eyes will always see, the best of EVERY circumstance;
To know there's nothing I will face, that happens just by chance!
Teach me very carefully, through ALL that comes my way;
To be conformed into YOUR image, Lord—with Contentment
  for Today!

FOLLOWING FOOTSTEPS

Trusting in answers, even when I can't SEE;
Walking by faith, in God's Will for ME!
Directed by passion and a love for the Lord;
Reaching to heaven, for His TRUE reward.
Following Jesus, as He leads the way;
Focused on Him, from the start of each day.
Tuned into HIS Spirit, yielded to hear;
Listening with patience, and waiting with cheer!
Following Footsteps—Lost in His Love;
Filled with His Peace and His Grace from above!

HIS TENDER SWEET COMPASSION

Sometimes I am unlovable , but I'm still precious in God's eyes;
For He sees PAST the hardness, to where my spirit lies.
He knows the hurts and heartaches, that have caused my life to
    change;
He knows what life has dealt, to bring such devastating pain!
So, with His Tender Sweet Compassion, He reaches out His hand;
He comforts and caresses, with a heart that understands.
His Tender Sweet Compassion, looks PAST, what my eyes see;
To the spirit man within me and what I'm called to BE!
With His Tender Sweet Compassion, He soothes my pain within;
He takes away, the heartache, and He breathes NEW life, AGAIN!
He wraps me up in loveliness, and puts His Fragrance within me;
He then opens heaven's doorway—and I'm released, to DESTINY!
There's abundance for my future, where NO good thing can be
    rationed;
It's in the Solace of His Presence—Dwelling IN His Sweet
    Compassion!

JUNE 30

ARMS OF GRACE

Lord, I bow my knee before You, in the struggles of each day;
Through the trials and tribulations, and each decision I will make.
When the fear is overwhelming, I know just WHERE to turn;
I'll place my eyes upon You, and give you my concerns!
My daily walk is rough, but You give light for each new day;
I know I couldn't make it, if You weren't there to guide my way.
There's a peace I have inside, just knowing You're with me;
It gives me hope for my tomorrows, and eyes that clearly see.
Lord, I know that I am covered, within the strength of Your
    embrace;
Safe within Your presence—and sheltered in Your Loving Grace!

JULY

STAYING ALIVE

(Read Job 1:8)

Lord, why do I have to suffer
The depth of deep heartache;
When I'm walking in Your promises
And standing strong in faith?
If you have chosen me for circumstance,
Or put a battle in my way;
May You sustain me in the process
And give me strength when I'm afraid?
For, Lord, I know it is NOT over
Until, YOU say, "It's done;"
So, I will look beyond the chaos
Until I have overcome!
The devil cannot kill me
For, You, Lord, own my life;
So, while I'm going through my "go through"
I'll trust in You, to stay alive.
Please, Lord, hold my mind together
And contain my every thought;
While I wait upon Your answers
And keep my eyes on You, Oh God!
So, though, the devil tries to slay me
I'll continue in the race;
Until this life is over,
And we are standing face to face!

HE HOLDS US IN HIS PROMISE

A teardrop falls from heaven and scatters as the dew;
With a blanket, ALL, is covered, washed clean and made brand
new.
With the fragrant breeze of wonder, the wind does gently blow;
And for a moment, heaven's portal, reveals the treasure His heart
holds.
Creation lies before Him, as far as any eye can see;
And He gathers up the ages and blesses all humanity.
For He sees PAST the horizons, of all the days gone by;
And watches most contently, what concerns both you and I.
He draws us to His bosom, at the dawn of each new day;
He breathes His breath within us and fills our hearts with praise.
He Holds Us in His Promise, inside the center of His Will;
And then releases us to walk, until our destiny's fulfilled.
He bestows upon us favor, like a Father to a son;
And He anoints us with His Spirit, to walk the path He's set us
on.
Yes, He opens heaven's portal at the dawn of each new day;
And He showers us with blessings, until our hearts are filled with
praise!

GOD'S MERCY EXTENDED

Lord, Your mercy extends every boundary and every limit of my
  mortal mind;
I cannot conceive its conception but stand amazed that it's,
  FOREVER, mine.
For You give a love that's unending and Your grace has been
  poured out on me;
My life testifies of Your greatness and I humble myself at Your
  feet.
Lord, it's Your promise to always sustain me, in the midst of all
  brimstone and fire;
When my enemy sets traps to ensnare me, and keep me bogged
  down in the mire.
It's that mercy that won't leave me hopeless, it rescues and draws
  me to You;
For, Lord, You are continually faithful, in all that I seem to go
  through.
You give me a secure habitation, to dwell in Your most secret
  place;
And it's under Your wings I take refuge—inside the sweet realm
  of Your grace.
I'm so grateful for the depth of Your mercy and the love You have
  lavished on me;
It's Your kindness that leads me to victory and surrenders my
  heart to Your peace!
Yes, it's Your Mercy Oh, God, Extended, that restores me and
  makes me whole;
It redeems me from what I DESERVE, and leaves me singing—
  "All's Well with My Soul."
Yes, Your mercy extends every boundary and every limit of my
  mortal mind;
I stand amazed at Your wondrous glory, and I receive it,
  FOREVER, as mine!

JULY 4

I Now Stand at a Fork in the Road

On the pathway of life I have taken
I find I have come to a Fork in the Road;
I'm in need, Lord, of Your Holy Spirit
To show me which way I should go.
For I know NOT which road I should travel—
I feel my life has just come to a halt;
I'm now faced with an uncertain journey
And I'm not sure where YOU'D have me to walk.
So, I petition You, Lord, for direction
For I've NO clue which choice to make;
I am desperate to hear from Your Spirit
As to exactly which road I should take.
Lord, I'll position myself to listen—
I will focus my heart upon You;
I will trust You to give me direction
And wisdom as to which path to choose.
Please, help me to make this decision
As I humble myself at Your throne;
Give me peace in the midst of transition
And YOUR grace to face the unknown.
Maneuver my heart, Lord, to follow
The way YOU would have me to go;
I pray for wisdom to make the right choice—
As I Now Stand at This Fork in the Road!

JULY 5

LOVE'S PASSION OUTPOURED

Breaking AND Blessing
Are EACH from the Lord;
They encumber our hearts
With Love's Passion Outpoured!
For God can give blessing
In the presence of loss;
To the one who draws close
And embraces the Cross.
It's Christ who stands ready
With arms open wide;
To comfort and soothe
The heartache inside.
You see, there's momentum in Him
Which gains strength through it all;
He's like the river that runs—
AFTER the fall!
Yes, breaking AND blessing
Will hold and they'll heal;
The heart that seeks Jesus
And HIS perfect will.
For the Lord will be there
No matter what you go through;
You're blessed when you've lost
What is MOST dear to you.
For it's THEN you draw in
And seek His embrace;
In the midst of the breaking
And the pain of heartache.
The key is in knowing
What's gained THROUGH the loss;
So waste NOT the sorrows
Of all that's been lost!

For breaking AND blessing
Are EACH from the Lord;
They encumber our hearts
With Love's Passion Outpoured.

HAND OF GOD

I have seen the Hand of God
When I didn't think I would;
I have watched Him move a mountain
And in awesome wonder STOOD!
I have witnessed His Sweet Spirit
Illuminate the darkest night;
I have seen Him touch the sparrow
And set her tiny wings to flight.
I have smelled the dainty fragrance
Of the flower in the field;
I have heard the baby's cry;
And I have seen the unsaved YIELD.
I have seen the winter and the spring time
The summer and the fall;
I have even looked inside myself
And seen the handprint of my God.
It's His voice in the whisper
And the sound of gentle rain;
It's the washing of His love
That comes and cleanses every stain.
It's the Hand of God that moves
When my eyes are fixed on Him;
It's His light inside the darkness
That resides as hope within.

HIS DANCE BECOMES MINE

May the face of my Jesus, be ALL that I see;
And hope from HIS heart, be planted in me.
May His passion and love, grab a hold of my soul;
And wash over so gently, from my head to my toes.
May my mindset be changed, so I'll always know;
That, no matter the struggle, He's STILL in control.
May HE be exalted to sit on the Throne;
In the realm of His Glory, where worship does flow!
I lift up my head and I look in HIS eyes;
His promise is mine—HE is my prize!
His face is before me, He is ALL that I see;
My heart grows not weary, because His eyes are on me!
He's my Glorious Treasure—His Love IS Divine;
My Life Now Is His—and HIS, Dance Becomes Mine!

BLOSSOM OF THE ROSE

The rose that blooms in springtime, is so awesome to behold;
It's exquisite in creation, as its tiny bud unfolds.
It radiates such beauty, with the smell of sweet perfume;
As the sun shines down upon it, and causes it to bloom.
It's like, it's gently kissed, and THEN it opens up in praise;
To give God all the Glory, as it stands in great array!
It's so extravagant in nature, to watch and see the rose;
Mature in awesome beauty, as its loveliness unfolds!
I cannot help but wonder, if this is what God sees;
When He gazes down from heaven and He stops and looks at me!
Does the beauty, He created, become a praise before His throne;
Have I matured, and become lovely—am I exquisite to behold?
Does the fragrance that I offer, smell like sweet perfume;
Has the tiny bud within me, yet, unfolded in full bloom?
Does my heart lift ever upward and erupt in heartfelt praise;
Do I stand in Heaven's Glory, completely clothed in great array?
Yes, I'm extravagant in nature, with awesome beauty to behold—
And when the Father looks upon me—He Beholds a Lovely Rose?

CONVICTIONS OF FAITH

I'm grasping for answers, struggling to win;
I'm caught in the warfare and the attacks from within.
I'm patiently waiting, for the victory to come;
And the manifestation, that the war has been won!
I'm facing each problem that seems to take hold;
With a peace and assurance, that God's in control.
His convictions of faith, have a grasp on my heart;
For I know that, in God, there is NOTHING too hard!
For each struggle I face, will soon fade away;
When I give them to Jesus, and let HIM lead the way.
Yes, God has a purpose and a plan for my life;
So, I'll yield to HIS ways—because they're HIGHER, than
  mine!

JULY 10

INSIDE HIS REALM OF GRACE

He quiets winds to whispers
He muzzles crashing waves;
His perfect peace is IN the storm—
Inside His Realm of Grace!
For He's resting in the center
And in Him there's calm within;
No lightening strikes to threaten
Nor noise of howling wind.
So, when the thunder rumbles
I'll know that God is near;
I'll not be tossed upon the waves
Nor swallowed up by fear.
I will turn to my Beloved
In the place where Glory dwells;
I will let HIM set my compass
And blow HIS wind upon my sails.
I will trust His EVERY promise
I'll keep my eyes upon the Lord;
I'll be completely safe in His boat—
For in Him, there is NO storm.

Finding Favor with God

I am a servant of the Most High God
My desire is for You, Lord, alone;
To You, be all glory and honor and power
FOREVER around heaven's throne!
Make me an instrument of Your hand—
An expression of Your heart in love;
May THIS vessel be found Kingdom worthy
As Your anointing flows out from above.
I stand and I ASK for Your blessings—
For ALL that's been stored up for me;
That I might walk in the favor of God
And in abundance—completely receive!
Enlarge the tent of my dwelling, Oh Lord,
Stir my heart with Your passion to see;
Give me courage and strength for each battle—
Send warring angels to keep evil from me.
May Your hand, Mighty God, come and rest
Upon my shoulders in such a great way;
That I'd truly be used for YOUR glory
And not have, or be used to cause pain.
Lord, I'm just a plain and simple servant
I'm nothing more—I'm nothing less;
Yet Your heart has heard my petition—
And You have granted my request!

SAFE WITHIN THE POTTER'S HANDS

I'm aware of all the changes, taking place upon the wheel;
I know the potter's molding by all the chipping that I FEEL.
But even in the midst of shaping, He is there to bring me through;
His hands are ever sculpting, to change MY point of view.
I am humbled in the process as He molds this piece of clay;
He's drawing out the nuggets and bringing beauty out of pain.
He pulls me from the fire when I put my trust in Him;
He exalts me in due season and lets me breathe again!
Never once am I alone, upon the potter's wheel;
I am safe within His hands—I'm being shaped to do His Will!

For a Moment I Stood in Glory

I turned and I looked toward heaven—
I saw such a magnificent light;
I knew right away it was Jesus
Telling me everything was all right.
It's as if my heart was drawn upward
To a realm where peace reigns supreme;
I then entered His Throne Room of Glory
MORE exquisite than I'd ever dreamed.
It was awesome to be in His presence
His life was the air that I breathed;
The fragrance of His Sweet Aroma
Completely filled up the inside of me.
My heart felt as if it would burst
I could feel HIS blood in my veins;
I joined with the heavenly angels
As they worshiped and offered Him Praise!
I knew beyond doubt of His Greatness
And the truth of ALL that He IS—
Yes, For a Moment I Stood in Glory
And I know now, Forever I'm His!

THE ANOINTING OF UNQUENCHABLE FIRE

The Anointing of Unquenchable Fire—
NOW, only an ember glows;
But SOON, its flame will ignite
And God's ultimate plan will unfold.
It is stoked by the Breath of His Spirit—
Fresh Fire for what lies ahead;
God's releasing His signs and His wonders
And HIS power to raise the dead!
The Anointing of Unquenchable Fire
Will be displayed before Nations and Kings;
Uniting God's love AND His holiness
And ALL that His promises bring.
The lost will be drawn by the fire
They will run to embrace its heat;
Hearts will be changed in a moment—
And humbly bow—at the Master's feet.
Angels are now loosed from heaven—
They carry hot coals in their hands;
They are touching the lips of the saints
And releasing revival AGAIN!
ASK and RECEIVE from the Father
Fresh Fire from heaven today;
For God is blowing the Breath of His Spirit—
To ignite and set embers ablaze!
By FAITH, receive every promise—
Let it become your heart's DEEP desire;
To walk where God calls you—with Power
And the Anointing of Unquenchable Fire!

ON THE WINGS OF AN EAGLE

God has raised you up on eagles' wings,
He has taught you how to fly;
He's held you up in the palm of His hand
And caused your life to shine.
He's helped you through each obstacle
And struggle you have faced;
He's guided you on the breath of dawn
And led you through by His grace.
He's anointed you with courage
And HIS strength to make it through;
Even when you felt you'd fall—
He was ALWAYS there for you.
For nothing you've experienced
Will ever be in vain;
God will never waste the heartache
Nor the grief that comes from pain.
Instead He gave you character
To achieve His highest goals;
And through your every trial
He's caused your faith to grow.
For it's in the midst of circumstance
That He enabled you to soar;
High above the jagged rocks
That line the canyon's floor.
It was faith in trusting Jesus
And HIS promises of love;
That held hope for new beginnings
When you felt like giving up.
It was He who lifted you on high
And made the darkness light,
And it's He who guides you, even now,
As you rise to meet new heights!

JULY 16

TENDER TOUCH OF JESUS

God not only sees the outside, but also what's within;
He knows the pain I've suffered, and He's aware of where I have
    been!
He has seen my wounded heart, that was so afraid to cry;
Because it hurt so deeply, that it felt as if I'd die!
He heard me in my quiet time, lifting up a prayer;
He saw my shoulders bent beneath, a burden of despair!
His heart, moved by compassion, and He breathed His breath on
    me;
He set His angels on assignment and He fought the enemy!
He opened heaven's window and poured His blessings from
    above;
He soothed my every heartache, and He wrapped me up in love!
The Tender Touch of Jesus, soothed and healed my every pain;
He washed away the turmoil with His ever gentle rain.
He restored to me, well being, and the peace I longed to know;
He filled me with His JOY and then He let me go!
I cannot help but stand amazed at ALL that He has done;
And I know down deep inside my heart, He's only just begun!
I'm now walking in His presence and my heart is filled with trust;
All Because of Sweet Compassion—and His Ever Gentle Touch!

JULY 17

My Life Is Yours to Hold

How can my words express the thoughts
Of all my heart can see;
How can I reach into the depths
And explain Your love for me?
For when I see the darkness—
You behold my soul;
You look past the weakness—
Into the treasure my heart holds.
It's there, beyond the realm of man
That I have eyes to see;
The Greatness of Your Glory
And all You've done for me.
So, even though, words can't express
What's buried deep within;
My spirit man rejoices
And I praise You once again.
It's knowing You are always there
That's music to my soul;
For MY destiny belongs to YOU—
And My Life Is Yours to Hold!

JULY 18

NEVER LOST FROM YOUR LOVE

(Read Psalm 139:1–12)

Oh Lord, You've examined my heart, and You know ALL there is
   to know;
You're aware when I stand or I sit, You observe when I come and
   go.
You know my every thought and deed, You've charted the path I
   would take;
EVERY moment, You know where I am, and every movement I'll
   ever make!
You know what I'm going to say, before I ever speak it aloud;
You know every thought I think, and every word that flows from
   my mouth.
It's too wonderful to even believe, that to YOU, Lord, I cannot be
   lost;
For I am always in Your presence—and I'm continually in Your
   thoughts!
I know, if I go up to heaven, You'll most assuredly be there;
Or if I ride on the morning winds, You will guide me with utter-
   most care.
Your strength will always support me, when the darkness tries
   most to befall;
The night will shine with Your light, and chase away, what's NOT
   of God!
There's not ONE place I can go, where You are NOT with me;
I cannot hide from Your Spirit, nor from Your holy presence, flee!
Constantly I am surrounded, caressed in Your peace from above;
I am safe and secure in Your presence
And I Am NEVER—Lost From Your Love!

WHAT SATAN MEANT FOR EVIL, JESUS MEANT FOR GOOD

Could mere words express an attitude
Or thoughts be put to rhyme;
To portray unbridled gratitude
Inside this grateful heart of mine?
For those who gave unselfishly
In the midst of deep despair;
To lift MY weight of heaviness
And share the burden I did bear.
To walk with me in crises
Through the dark night of my soul;
Brightly shining forth a beacon
Upon my long and dreary road.
For only in the silence
Could my heart completely see;
The Miracle of Friendship
And ALL you truly mean to me.
Yes, you've been the silver lining
In a cloud laced with despair;
You've encouraged me with love
By just ALWAYS being there!
I look around and all I see
Is God's handiwork displayed;
My darkness turned to light—
And precious lives completely changed.
Now I stand within God's presence
With HIS promise understood;
You see, What Satan Meant for Evil
My Loving Jesus Meant for Good!

THE GOD OF MY BREAKTHROUGH

God has something even greater than what I'm walking in today;
So my heart is reaching out and I'm standing strong in faith.
I'm rising up in boldness, in the authority of Christ;
For you see, I'm on a mission, and my dream is close in sight.
I WILL fulfill the vision and my spirit WILL arise;
Because I know I'm on the threshold of a breakthrough in my life.
I'll daily keep my focus upon the Lord alone;
And I'll speak only words of faith and break frustration's hold.
You see, the testing of my faith produces patience in my life;
So, I WON'T give in to fear, instead I'll stand and fight.
I'll press in more and more to Jesus, I will seek and I'll pursue
And I'll Forever Keep My Eyes upon, the God of My
   Breakthrough!

JULY 21

MEASURE OF GRACE

There is a Measure of Grace that only God can extend;
It has unlimited boundaries and consuming love without end.
It brings both comfort and peace to hearts ravaged by loss;
It draws those who are hurting to the foot of the Cross.
For, it's the Lord's tender touch that will stir and renew;
When emotions are shattered, broken, tattered and bruised.
He is the hope for the hopeless, He's the beginning and end;
The very source of our strength, that resides deep within.
It's the faith in our Lord that will lead us through;
When the hardships of life come to overpower and pursue.
For Christ is the Rock on which we must fall;
In the midst of the storm and the face of it all.
He will always be there like an anchor that holds;
He'll send His Sweet Holy Spirit to gently love and console.
It's HIS Measure of Grace that He extends from above;
That will soothe, calm and heal and wash over with love!

OUR DESTINY

Greatness lies within each heart, and in its ability to see;
ALL, that God has destined, in His plan for you and me.
At the moment, His breath of life, surged inside our souls;
He planted seeds for Glory and left them there to grow.
Yes, He merely breathed and He created, all we'd ever be;
In an instant, life began, and He became Our Destiny.
He bestowed, to each, a purpose, and gifts to help us through;
And then He placed us in our journey, to do what we were called
    to do.
Every human being, holds the greatness of our God;
Unique in every aspect, with a purpose and a call.
If only hearts could see, what's planted deep within;
They would know they were created for a most specific plan.
Yes, greatness lies within each heart—if only we could know;
That God's STILL there, to breathe upon, the seeds within our
    souls.
In the midst of transformation, we'd be all we're called to be;
For we would have our eyes on Jesus and, HE, would be Our
    Destiny!

ROADWAY TO THE CROSS

If we focus on the problem, instead of on the goal;
We'll find ourselves off balance and reeling from the blow.
You see, we cannot make decisions based on emotions deep
within;
We cannot overcome adversity, until we're truly seeking HIM!
Our hope must be positioned upon the precious grace of God;
Our hearts must find humility or pride will cause a fall.
We must face each fear with boldness and not forget the truth
we've heard;
We MUST trust the Lord, by faith, and stand upon His Word.
When we learn to persevere, we'll learn to truly overcome;
When we stand AGAINST the odds, we'll surely hear the words,
"Well Done!"
God has called us to a journey, He has equipped us for the race;
Adversity should ONY show us, the steadfast love of God's
embrace.
The truth is—we will ALWAYS win, even when we've felt we've
lost;
If the path we choose to follow, is the Roadway to the Cross.
Dear Saint of God, keep going, continue steadfast in the race;
Set your compass bound for Glory, and Your heart upon His
Face!

JULY 24

HIS PROMISE IN THE TESTING

Prairie fires burn, consuming all that's in their way;
And the harshness of the summer winds make no way of escape.
The trail of billowing smoke ascends, to kiss the pale blue sky;
Leaving patchwork quilts of darkness upon the tattered land-
    scape's pride.
But in the devastating loss, life will always find a way;
To endure the test of fire and hell's all-consuming blaze.
For death cannot extinguish what is only God's to hold;
It Is His Promise in the Testing—to bring us forth as gold.
I find it's only IN the fire that we can truly see His face;
When we run without pretense, into His presence and embrace.
Yes, it often takes the fire, to give us eyes to see;
His plan within the trial, designed for you and me.
So when the winds blow fiercely and the fire rages on;
May we persevere in victory, until the battle has been won.
Men will know we're overcomers by the way we trust and cope;
When they're standing close beside us and all that's left is smoke.
It's our triumph in the kingdom, it's our hope in Him alone;
It IS His Promise in the Testing—to bring us forth as gold!

However, the spiritual is not first, but the natural, and
afterward the spiritual.
—1 CORINTHIANS 15:46

I'LL MAKE MY LIFE
AN OFFERING

It is MY desire, to be a vessel for the King;
To humbly bow before Him and Make My Life an Offering.
But often I'm blindsided and my feet become unsure;
My walk's not always steady, nor my motives always pure.
I need the Holy Spirit to clean me up and make me new;
To wash and cleanse my heart—touch my spirit and renew.
To open heaven's portal that I might enter in;
To a place inside God's Glory, where I can worship Him.
I know His Love is faithful and forever will endure;
Even in MY times of weakness when I'm shaky and unsure.
So, I will put my eyes on Jesus and NOT the obstacles I face;
My heart will find its focus upon the One who gives me grace.
For, I am but a vessel, designed to glorify my King;
So, in His presence, I will bow, and Make My Life an Offering.

JULY 26

HEART EXPRESSIONS

Expressions of the heart, often minister within;
They're the gifts God gladly gives, when we put our trust in Him.
Each expression of the heart, has so many things to share;
Touching others' lives, healing wounds that may be there.
Heart Expressions bring excitement, to those with ears to hear;
Always pointing toward the Master, reminding—He is ALWAYS
    near.
To know the Lord will minister, no matter WHAT the need;
Brings comfort in the struggle, and such soothing inner strength.
For, love within the heart, holds boundaries without end;
It's beyond the price of gold—when it truly comes from Him!

JULY 27

PREPARE FOR KINGDOM GLORY

Let all the earth give praise, as we stand before the King;
May we lift our hands in worship, as our hearts begin to sing!
For, God has heard the cries, of His people in their plight;
And He's approaching, with a vengeance—He's turning all the
    wrong to right!
He's seen us in our time of need, He's ALWAYS been aware;
And, NOW, He is releasing, answers to our prayers.
For what we've sown, we'll surely reap—and we will truly be
    amazed;
To watch God's Hand, in action—as He Works in Mighty Ways!
Heaven's doors have NOW been opened ,and God's declaring
    WAR—
So, Prepare for Kingdom Glory and EVERY Promise of Reward!

JULY 28

WHERE IS MY BELOVED?

Where Is My Beloved—
He said He would not leave;
Yet, I cannot seem to see Him
Nor smell Him in the air I breathe.
I am searching for His presence
In this hostile barren land;
But it appears He's simply vanished
And has forgotten who I am.
I cry to Him in darkness
And bid Him to my side;
In anguish my heart's breaking
For fear of being left behind.
Where Is My Beloved—
Will He ever come again;
Will He tend my broken heart
And mend it from within?
Is He calling me to rise ABOVE
What I am prone to SEE and HEAR;
And trust Him in His promise
That He is always near?
For when I seek Him, I will find Him
And in the process grow;
And when it's all been said and done
I'll find I NEVER was alone.
Where Is My Beloved—
He is ALWAYS close to me;
Even when I cannot see Him
Nor smell Him in the air I breathe.
For My Beloved will NOT leave me
Instead He waits for ME to come;
With outstretched arms He beckons
And woos me gently by His love!

JULY 29

ALWAYS HERE

You need not worry anymore—for I am ALWAYS near;
I won't leave you, nor forsake you—yes, I Am Always Here!
I'm close at hand to listen, when you feel you're all alone;
I'm your place of peaceful refuge, I'm your all-consuming hope!
I am your inner strength, I'm the Spirit that abides;
I'm your safe place in the struggle, where you can run and hide.
I'm your shoulder in the darkness, I'm ALL you'll ever need;
I'm your joy in the journey, I'm the light that guides your feet.
Yes, I am ALWAYS with you, in your laughter or your tears;
And I will NEVER leave you—my Child, I Am Always Here!

BOUNTY OF THE BLESSING

Your prayers have reached the ear, of the Father up above;
And He's granted each request, with His everlasting love.
The Bounty of the Blessing, will abundantly exceed;
Everything that you have prayed for and every heartfelt need.
The Bounty of the Blessing comes directly from His Throne;
Through the sound of thunderous waters, in a mighty river's flow.
Yes, the Bounty of the Blessing, has been sent for you to see;
God's purpose and His plan and your awesome destiny!
For your prayers have reached His ear, and He is pouring forth;
The anointing of His Spirit, and new hope from heaven's shore;
So, lift your heart before Him, in order to receive;
The Bounty of the Blessing, and the harvest of the seed!

July 31

Wind Beneath My Wings

God's Spirit is the Power—
He's the Wind Beneath My Wings;
He carries me to places
And He shows me hidden things.
His purpose in my life
Is to rise above the clouds;
Upon the thermal of His presence
High above the busy crowd.
In the realm of revelation
In the Glory of the Lord;
Is where His Spirit takes me—
It's where He beckons me to soar.
You see, He's called me like an eagle
And has set my wings to flight;
He breathes His breath upon me
And He teaches me to fly.
Yes, God's Spirit IS the Power—
He's the Wind Beneath My Wings;
And He carries me to places
That far exceed my wildest dreams.

Face to Face with God

My God's Still in Control

Firm Foundation

It Ain't Over 'Til It's Over

Treasure in the Trial

No Limits

Dance of the Dance, Song of All Songs

His Glory to Behold

Living Water

The Victory Is Yours to Receive

Angels Among Us

All-Sufficient Grace

His Breath of Song in Praise

Kingdom Pursuit

Passion of God's Love

Forever Loved As Your Own

Captivate My Heart

The Wonders of His Glory

Valley Floor

God of the Impossible

Purpose in the Desert

Summer Season

Beyond Myself to Victory

He Is Ever Faithful in All Concerning Me

Let Your Mercy Fall

Through Heaven's Eyes

Lighthouse on a Hill

Rainbow's End

Living Life on Purpose

Foundation Stones

Heaven's Shore

August 1

Face to Face with God

If I could climb to higher heights, without the fear I'd fall;
Then surely I would know the depth and the majesty of God.
For, it's only in the incline that I'll have eyes to see;
His mighty hand extended—reaching down to rescue me!
Finding favor in the promise of ALL, He said He'd do;
Seeking peace within the solace—trusting Him to see me
     through.
To give up would be so foolish when I'm this close to the top;
I can almost see the summit and I can smell the breath of God.
He summons me to rise above—He gives me courage for the
     climb;
For it's the Treasure of His Presence that I truly seek to find.
So, I'll continue in my journey without the fear I'll fall;
Until my heart's been raptured and I am Face to Face with God!

MY GOD'S STILL IN CONTROL

I refuse to walk in darkness—AWAY from truth and light;
No matter what the world brings, through its arrogance and lies.
I will not be deceived, by those sent to lead astray;
For, God's anointing is upon me, to the lies that they portray.
My heart will never compromise, nor will I let the lies uproot—
For the convictions deep within me are directed to seek truth
So, when anyone comes to me, proclaiming the gospel as it's not;
I'll stand my ground, unwavering—upon the Word of God.
Yes, until the end, I'll stand, contending for the faith;
I will love what my God loves and I will hate what my God hates.
I will never choose the darkness and compromise my life
Instead, my passion will burn brightly for my love of Jesus Christ.
And then one day, the time will come—to stand before the Lord;
And I will know I've done my best as a soldier in this war.
For God knows what I am made of and so I can't help but expose;
The spirit of deception and his plan as it unfolds.
You see, the light will always conquer what the darkness tries to
   hold
So, I will rest assured in knowing that My God's Still in Control.

AUGUST 3

FIRM FOUNDATION

When the raging storms I face
Expose me for what I am;
Will I find myself upon the Rock
Or upon the sinking sand?
Will I find I'll have endurance
When the storm is most severe;
Or will I just crumble and give up
And be blown away by fear?
For the storms of life will truly show
What's hidden in my soul—
Will I withstand the blowing winds
That toss me to and fro?
It's Only by the Grace of God
That I will find the faith to stand;
Securely anchored to the Lord—
Holding tightly to HIS hand.
For it's only when I build upon
The Firm Foundation of the Lord;
That I will find myself still standing
Through the wrath of any storm!

IT AIN'T OVER 'TIL IT'S OVER

Deep calls unto deep, in the roar of waterfalls;
And hope rest in the Spirit, through the light inside of God.
There's anointing deep within, that pushes men to grow;
With a catapult of thrust, toward the promises God holds.
It's when a soul does truly thirst, for the depths of ALL God has;
Where strength becomes a pedestal, and HIS prize is there to
    grab!
It's peace within the storm, when the waves are crashing in;
It's standing strong in faith, no matter WHERE you've been.
Yes, it's resting in His shadow, until His mighty hand does move;
With the knowledge —It Ain't Over, UNTIL, He Brings You
    Through!

TREASURE IN THE TRIAL

Treasures can be found in darkness
If you should ONLY seek to find;
For pearls come out of trials
And pain that try to bind.
Darkness cannot hold a saint
For the WORD is plain and clear;
That ALL things work for good
To those with ears to hear.
So, in every single circumstance
That seems to bring defeat;
Remember that the human heart
Has such extraordinary strength.
Look within the darkness
PAST the heartache, fear and pain;
Find the Treasure in the Trial
Through the light of Christ that reigns.
For the loving Savior always knows
That treasures will be found;
When we look past every circumstance
That tries so hard to hold us down.

NO LIMITS

I could never think or dream
Or ever dare come close;
To the plan that Jesus has for me
Or what my future holds.
Far beyond my comprehension
Of what mere eyes can see;
God will do EXCEEDINGLY above
All that I could ever think.
For EVERYTHING is possible
From the Father's point of view;
NOTHING is too hard for Him—
There's not a thing He cannot do.
MY mind has limitations
That find dreams hard to comprehend;
But the mind of God is limitless—
It has boundaries without end.
If I could only learn to trust
With a heart of faith to see;
That my God has NO LIMITS
In His plans concerning me!

AUGUST 7

DANCE OF THE DANCE, SONG OF ALL SONGS

You're the Dance of the Dance and the Song of All Songs;
The love of my life—You're the beat that goes on.
You're the musician who plays my heartstrings of love;
Like a heavenly instrument strummed from above.
You're my precious beloved to whom I'm betrothed;
You're the blood in my veins and the breath in my soul.
You're the Dance of the Dance and the Song of All Songs;
You're the lead that I follow as we dance until dawn.
You're God's melody singing a special love song to me;
As You whisper so gently—"Come Dance with Me"
Yes, You're the Dance of the Dance and the Song of All Songs;
You are the love of my life—to Whom my heart belongs!

AUGUST 8

HIS GLORY TO BEHOLD

He stirs the depths of oceans,
He puts the froth upon the wave;
He places stars in heaven,
And puts their brilliance on display.
He covers lofty mountain peaks
With blankets of fresh snow;
And in the shadows of the moonlight
He gives His Glory to Behold!
He puts His setting sun
Upon the distant shore;
He shades the scorching desert,
And gives relief until the morn.
He breathes upon the earth
And covers it with dew;
He opens up the wilderness
And makes a road to travel through.
His majesty is wondrous,
His love will not grow old;
He paints His beauty on earth's canvas
And gives His Glory to Behold!

AUGUST 9

LIVING WATER

In the sorrow of the mourning when my heartache's so surreal;
I'll search to find God's comfort by digging deeper in the well.
For, inside is Living Water that only Christ can give;
It's His portion in my crisis and His love that lives within.
It fills the empty spaces and every crevasse of my soul;
It's like healing balm from heaven that swiftly flows from head to
    toe.
It's a treasure that is timeless with no beginning and no end;
It's the comfort of God's Spirit that's faithful time and time again.
So, when I'm feeling overwhelmed, I will look into His face;
My heart will find its focus upon His love and grace.
And I'll know His Living Water will refresh, heal and renew;
In the sorrow of the mourning and every THING that I go
    through!

AUGUST 10

THE VICTORY IS YOURS TO RECEIVE

Come AND Walk on the Water with Me—
For I'm stretching YOUR faith to see;
PAST all that would cause you to fear
And keep you from trusting in ME!
For even in times when you feel you will fall
My hand will reach in and retrieve;
Pulling you safe from the turbulent waves
In the midst of the perilous sea.
You see, the victory IS yours, if you'll only believe—
Merely stretch forth your hand and receive;
For there's nothing that I wouldn't do for you
When the eyes of your heart are on, ME!
So, COME, and Walk on the Water,
Unafraid of the tumultuous sea;
Take hold of the promise before you—
My Child, the Victory Is YOURS to Receive!

AUGUST 11

ANGELS AMONG US

Mingled in among us, are angels from above;
Dispersed by God's own hand, sent to minister HIS love.
The angelic heavenly beings give instruction, lead and guide;
They go beyond the realm of man, and what we witness with our
eyes.
Some deliver us from trouble as they stand and fight warfare;
Others come to meet our needs, disguised as angels unaware!
God has given us His angels as we travel through this land;
To help keep us on His path and follow His commands.
He's sent His angels in among us, to direct us on our way;
To watch over every step, protect and keep us safe.
They almost always go unseen as they maneuver to and fro;
You see, their focus is ABOVE—they merely do what they are
told.
But every now and then, we're allowed a glimpse of them;
To remind us of the Father's grace and direct our eyes to HIM!
Yes, angels are among us, sent directly from above;
To guide us safely on our journey, until our life on earth is done!

AUGUST 12

ALL-SUFFICIENT GRACE

Troubles roll in like morning dew, they surround and encumber
    me;
The darkness wraps itself around, 'til I can scarcely breathe.
I fight so hard to stay alive, but it's hard to make it through.
For I'm often focused on the trial, instead of looking , Lord,
    toward YOU!
I'm not always standing strong in faith, I find myself in fear;
I cannot hush the constant lies, that whisper in my ear.
The battle rages fiercely on, between my heart and mind;
The lies try to confuse, steal my hope and leave me blind.
Oh God, I need Your eyes to see, and Your arms to envelope me;
I need Your peace amidst this storm, and YOUR hand to calm the
    sea.
I need to feel Your presence, and Your courage when I am weak;
To stand inside Your shadow, and walk within Your strength.
I ask for grace to make it through, even when I cannot see;
When darkness seems to cover, and wrap its ugly arms round me.
I ask for faith to take the steps, that lead me through this trial;
Even when I'm truly overwhelmed, help me go that extra mile.
Because I know that in the end, I will understand it all;
I'll see that You were always there, and You never let me fall.
Help me learn, Lord, in the storm, even when I cannot see;
That Your grace is All Sufficient, with outstretched arms of love
    for me!

HIS BREATH OF SONG IN PRAISE

In God's hands are held the depths
Of the earth and of the seas;
He formed the river beds
And fashioned lofty mountain peaks.
He is robed in royal majesty
He is ever armed with peace;
The heaven's and the earth are HIS—
There's not a thing outside His reach.
He shines His light upon the day
And watches o'er the night;
He kisses morning with the dew—
He puts the sparkle in the stars so bright!
His creation is HIS ornament
His Breath of Song in Praise;
Adorned to bring Him GLORY—
FOREVER and ALWAYS!

AUGUST 14

KINGDOM PURSUIT

Kingdom Pursuit to the valley's end
Through obstacles large and small;
Fighting for victory no matter what
Rising up after every fall.
Searching for answers that cannot be seen
In a realm where the angels fight;
Trusting in Jesus though the heavens seem closed
And waiting for even one glimmer of light.
Yes, pursuing the Kingdom and not giving up
Running the race to the end;
Persevering with vigor the journey of faith
And believing God's promises hidden within.
Keeping eyes focused and set on the Lord
In the midst of all that may come;
With hope for tomorrow and peace for today
Until life on this earth is done!

Passion of God's Love

Set my heart aflame, Oh God
And seal it with Your love;
Burn within, YOUR passion,
And reveal Your healing touch.
Don't define me by my struggles, Lord
Instead, peer deep within;
To the heart BEHIND the weakness
And my sorrow over sin.
May my heart be filled with love
Redeemed to sing Your praise;
And may my worship be extravagant
As I stand at heaven's gate.
May the passion of YOUR love
Burn deep within my soul;
Quench NOT Your holy fire
Instead refine me as pure gold!
Pursue me for Your Kingdom
And capture me today;
Place Your seal upon my heart
And take me prisoner Lord, I pray!

AUGUST 16

FOREVER LOVED AS YOUR OWN

May the life of Your Spirit come alive within me;
That I might grow in Your love and stand pure before Thee!
With a heart that is focused to faithfully see;
That it's all about YOU, Lord, it is NOT about me!
For ALL that will happen in my life today;
Has been set by Your compass to show me YOUR way.
The direction I'm headed and this road I now trod;
Is merely my pathway ,into Your presence, Oh God.
So, I ask that You'll give me, ALL I will need;
From this point on, until my journey's complete.
And when I've arrived at the gates of Your Throne;
May I bask in Your Glory and be—
Forever Loved As Your Own!

CAPTIVATE MY HEART

Captivate My Heart, Oh God,
Apprehend my mind;
Orchestrate YOUR thoughts in me
So that they are mine.
Change my every attitude
Until I'm just like You;
Conformed into YOUR image
By ALL I say and do.
Help me understand YOUR ways
And Your call upon my life;
Anoint me with Your Spirit, Lord
And give me wings to fly.
Activate my senses
And stir each gift within;
Reproduce YOUR Holiness
And revive me once again.
Open up my vision, Lord,
So I can clearly see;
The heart behind my Father
And Your loving thoughts toward me.
Permeate my being—
Consume my heart I pray;
Produce fire from Your Spirit
To burn all the chaff away.
Emerge to be victorious
Through the abandonment I give;
Equip me to walk within Your Grace
And teach me DAILY how to live.
Use me for Your Glory
To advance Your Kingdom, Lord;
Give me wisdom on my journey
And a heart to trust You MORE!

THE WONDERS OF HIS GLORY

I looked upward, into heaven, and saw the opening of a door;
I beheld a blazing light, coming down, to touch earth's floor.
In the shimmer of its gleaming, I saw angelic host descend;
And in an instant, darkness vanished, by the blowing of God's
    wind.
It's as if ALL time stood silent, and everything in sight;
Was washed in brilliant color, as it came into the light!
I heard the Father's voice, like a mighty thunderous roar;
Releasing depths of revelation, that I had NEVER known before.
I felt as if I'd crumble, beneath the splendor of it all;
But I didn't want to MISS—this outpouring of my God!
You see, for such a time as this, He opened heaven's door;
And shined His light directly, upon creation's floor.
I have witnessed Kingdom Glory, as He opened up the sky;
And I saw the brilliant colors, shining forth from Heaven's Light.
Yes, God caressed this earthly body and gave me eyes to SEE;
The Wonder's of His Glory and His Love That Washes Me!

VALLEY FLOOR

It's been awhile, My child, since you sensed My Spirit near;
But even in your valley's lowest, I've seen your every tear.
Each were captured in a bottle, as My heart reached out to you;
But you couldn't FEEL, My presence, in what you were going
     through.
I whispered songs of comfort, to calm your raging soul;
To soothe the savage beast, that had come to take control.
If you could only understand that this trial was meant to bring;
Hope for NEW tomorrows and amazing inner strength.
You see, without the valley's lowest, you'd never know the
     mountaintop;
You would never understand, the depth of heaven's walk.
But, STILL, you often felt alone, and were convinced I did not
     care;
You had no clue, that ALL the time, I was there with you.
My child, you learned so many things, upon the Valley Floor;
And I know someday you'll thank me, for all that you endured.
But until then, I hope you'll know, how much I care for you;
May you know I'm ALWAYS there—no matter WHAT, you're
     going through!

AUGUST 20

GOD OF THE IMPOSSIBLE

I am the God of the Impossible, and I'm just as close as any
    prayer;
I hear each request that you have made, and assign My angels
    there.
It truly matters to My heart, what stirs within your soul;
It's My desire to meet your needs, and let My blessings flow.
You think in darkness I can't see, the place where your heart
    hides;
But I've heard your pleas of agony, and brought deliverance to
    your life.
You see, I could move a mountain, if it was needed to answer
    prayer;
For there is nothing you will ever face, that will catch me
    unaware.
So never think I do not hear, the heartfelt prayers of faith;
Trust Me to hold your heart and soul, just stand my child and
    wait.
My miracles are coming, lift your face, trust Me and see;
Remember, I can do ALL things—
For there's NOTHING that's too hard for Me!

PURPOSE IN THE DESERT

God often takes me through the desert
So He can bring me to my knees;
He puts me in positions
Where I have to stop and look at ME!
And when I finally reach that realm
Where I'm at the end of self;
It's then He picks me up
And offers me HIS help.
He opens up my eyes
So I can clearly see;
HIS purpose for the desert
And HIS plans concerning me.
He brings me to a place
Where the ONLY way is HIM;
And then He guides me on my journey
By extending forth His hand.
So I AM forever grateful
Because the desert helps me see;
All that God is doing
In order to change ME!

AUGUST 22

SUMMER SEASON

I've planted seed in drought times when I could not smell the
    rain;
I've watched the storm clouds gather but still my faith remained.
I've adjusted to the summer's heat and long hours into night;
I have wearied through exhaustion but I've continued in my
    plight.
Yes, the seed I've sown seems endless but I've yet to see the crop;
For it's hard to SEE the harvest when the ground is hard as rock.
You see, the season of the summer is work from dawn to dark;
And often times relentless—a dry and dusty work of art
But the harvest follows summer and that seed within the soil;
Will flourish in the sunshine, amidst the sweat and toil.
Yes, there's a promise of the harvest and its blessings will be seen;
When the crop comes to fruition and yields abundance from
    each seed.
So when the ground is hardened and weathered by harsh storms;
May I understand God's process and trust the harvest, to the
    Lord!

BEYOND MYSELF TO VICTORY

My warfare has been crazy, and sometimes knocks me off my
    guard;
I have attacks upon my life, that take their hold upon my heart.
But, I've learned that opposition will tip me off to who I am;
Even WHEN the devil's mad, and wants to come and steal my
    land.
You see, God has placed within me, a mighty rushing wind;
He's gifted me for service—to live my life, in HIM.
So, even in the winepress when I'm hiding from the Lord;
He still pursues me for His army, and He gives me wings to soar.
He calls me PAST myself, so He can activate my faith;
He gives me what I need, to boldly walk out of the cave.
Yes, He always has a plan, even when I have NO clue;
For, He knows WHERE I am going and He knows what I can do.
So, in the midst of warfare, when the storm is bearing down;
When the battle lines are drawn and the answers can't be found,
I will turn my eyes to heaven, I will stand and fight the war;
I'll go Beyond Myself, TO Victory—and give my battles to the
    Lord!

AUGUST 24

HE IS EVER FAITHFUL IN ALL CONCERNING ME

God's blessing is upon me—His favor is my cloak.
His Glory is my portion and His vision is my hope.
His provision is my gift in the season of His Grace,
His benefits flow freely and become my warm embrace.
His Word is my perspective that keeps my heartbeat calm,
His promises are sure and carry healing balm.
His very love's my passion, His breath's the air I breathe;
Yes, He Is Ever Faithful in ALL concerning me.

AUGUST 25

LET YOUR MERCY FALL

I cry for mercy, mercy, mercy, when my heart in turmoil screams;
I cry for mercy, mercy, mercy, and the healing mercy brings.
For when the mercy of my Jesus is showered from above;
I can rest in arms of angels, cradled safe within His love.
I cry for mercy, mercy, mercy, to fall like morning dew;
To saturate my broken heart—restore and make it new.
I cry for mercy, mercy, mercy, when I've nothing left to give;
Except this cry upon my heart, and these words upon my lips.
For it's the mercy of my Father, that will find me in my need;
It's the mercy He pours forth, that I desire and humbly seek.
I cry for mercy, mercy, mercy, from the mercy seat of God;
Lord, I pray, You hear my prayer, and Let Your Mercy Fall!

THROUGH HEAVEN'S EYES

To think that when You see me, what You gaze upon is pure;
To know You look with passion and a consuming love that will
  endure.
For You don't look upon the darkness that MY earthly eyes
  behold;
Instead You look with YOUR eyes, past the grip of this world's
  hold.
You see the preciousness of life and a heart of love for You;
It's like when deep calls unto deep—it's like the kiss of morning
  dew.
It's when Your awesome Holy Spirit comes and dwells within my
  life;
That I can more clearly understand that You don't look with
  earthly eyes.
For your desire is to love me, in the midst of where I am;
To pursue with holy passion, this frailty of man.
You go beyond the outer boundaries to the very depth that lies
  within;
It's the YES within my spirit, that you seek Your interest in.
It's my heart that YOU pursue, not this earthly world's disguise;
Lord, You don't see what MAN sees—instead, You see Through
  Heaven's Eyes!

Lighthouse on a Hill

In the midst of darkness, a tiny light appeared—
Like the flickering of a candle's burning flame;
As I focused on the light inside the night,
The perspective of my life began to change.
The light then exploded upon the darkness,
And illuminated the black and gloomy skies;
The light just seemed to pierce through the darkness,
Giving brand new direction and guidance to my life.
So, I set the compass of my heart to leave the darkness,
And pursue the light that now stretched out before;
I finally had a destination my heart could follow—
I was now headed in the direction of the Lord.
NOW, I can see the Lighthouse on the Hill,
With its beam shining out to find the lost;
Drawing those who've been swallowed by the darkness
To the light of Christ upon the Cross.
It's the Lighthouse on the Hill that won't be hidden,
For it is the LIFE of Christ that truly IS the light;
It's the Holy Spirit that resides within God's saints,
Standing firm and doing battle through the night.
It's the Lighthouse on the Hill that gave direction
When I was lost and could not find MY way;
When I was wandering without hope amidst the darkness,
It was the lighthouse that led me safely to His grace.
Now I pray that I, myself, will never hide
The light of Jesus that burns within my life;
For there are others who are lost inside the darkness
That will need a light to follow in the night.
May God use me as a Lighthouse on a Hill
With HIS light to pierce the darkest night;
May others find their way to follow Jesus—
Through the light of Christ that burns within my life!

AUGUST 28

RAINBOW'S END

It isn't always easy to SEE the Rainbow's End;
Nor the reward of final outcome, when you only just begin.
For the pathway of your choosing often brings with it potholes;
But it's the struggles of the journey, that will cause your life to
    grow.
It's dedication to achieve and persevere with inner strength;
Even when the road is rocky and you feel so frail and weak.
And then one day you'll see the SON emerging through life's
    storms;
As you focus on the Rainbow's End and the fruit of its rewards.
You'll see the character instilled in you along life's rocky road;
Has truly brought more value than fine riches, jewels or gold.
You'll find rewards of TRUE success, when you reach the
    Rainbow's End;
By looking for the pot of gold, with eyes that look WITHIN!

Living Life on Purpose

The Father has intended
That I should live abundantly in HIM;
So I Am Living Life on Purpose,
From the beginning to the end.
You see, MY life WAS created,
With a purpose and a plan;
My Father called me by my name
And He formed me with HIS hand.
I'm NOT under limitations
Of this world and what is said;
For I'm living in HIS presence
Redeemed and loved instead!
I WILL live the way HE tells me,
No matter how I FEEL;
Because I belong to HIM
And my heart's received His seal.
Yes, I am soaking in His Spirit,
I'm filled with joy, hope and peace;
I Am Living Life on Purpose,
Safe within the Master's reach.

AUGUST 30

FOUNDATION STONES

God's foundations teach me principles
That DAILY help me grow;
His basic truths become my catalyst
Thrusting me to heights unknown.
HIS foundations are my launching pad,
They help me rise above—
Every obstacle and roadblock
Or whatever ELSE may come.
They position me for GREATER things
In the Kingdom of the Lord;
They stretch my every fiber
To believe for even MORE!
Foundation Stones will NOT shift
They're secure and strong in God;
You see, my life's not built upon the sand—
It Is Built upon the Rock!
I am headed toward perfection
I will NOT linger in dead works;
I am listening to His Spirit
And standing strong upon His Word.
My heart has found its focus—
I'm planted firm on solid ground;
MY House Is Built upon the Rock—
And it will NOT tumble down!

August 31

Heaven's Shore

Lord, can I ride the wave to Glory, that comes inside the storm;
Will I have an awesome story, when I land on Heaven's Shore?
Will the love You freely offer, completely fill me up with peace;
Even when I'm being tossed about, upon the raging sea?
Will the boat I'm in, be sturdy—will it withstand the hopeless
    night;
Can I trust that You will keep me, until the morning light?
Lord, will You be my portion—can I wait until the dawn;
Will I trust You, in Your promise, to turn my chaos, into calm?
Will I surf atop ascending waves, until I reach sand-covered
    shores;
Will I have the strength to rise above, and live for YOU, Oh Lord?
And when the storm clouds gather and pour torrential rains;
Will I find myself inside Your peace and lost in Your embrace?
For in tumultuous times, Oh Lord—will I find I cling to hope;
Knowing You will NEVER leave me—afraid, lost or alone?
Will I trust Your EVERY promise, will I keep my eyes on You;
Will I hang on until tomorrow—knowing YOU, will see me
    through?
Will I ride the wave to Glory that comes inside the storm;
Lord, will I have an awesome story, when I land on Heaven's
    Shore?

Glory's Sweet Dew

Through Spirit Eyes

Keeper of the Light

Behind the Wheel

Only in You Will I Make It

Peace Within the Storm

The Mouth of the Lion Has Opened and
He's Releasing a Mighty Roar

A Beam of Heaven's Glory

The Race Is Almost Over

Sweet Lord

To Behold the Light of Your Face

Wings of a Dove

Clinging to the Cross

Shelter in the Storm

His Kiss Upon My Face

Apple of God's Eye

Upon the Potter's Wheel

Footstool of the Throne

Purified Gold

My Life Is but a Journey

The Treasure His Heart Holds

Season of Your Grace

My Song to Him

Polished Gem

Life's Not Perfect

Send Your Love

Kingdom Vision

Wings of Prayer

The Beauty of His Masterpiece

The Seasons of a Life

SEPTEMBER 1

GLORY'S SWEET DEW

Oh God, who am I that You are mindful of me;
With a love that is greater than what my earthly eyes see?
Yes, who am I, Lord, that You would draw me so close;
To be enveloped in mercy and surrounded with hope?
Who am I, Lord in the midst of it all;
To walk in Your presence and call You, my God?
Oh Lord, who am I, on earth's blissful shore;
To hear the sound of Your voice as You summon me forth?
YES, Who Am I, Lord—except a mirror of YOU;
Lovingly washed in the fragrance of Glory's Sweet Dew!

THROUGH SPIRIT EYES

Lord, You have fashioned all my days, You hold the blueprints of
  my life;
You've established me in truth and imparted greatness deep
  inside.
You've fulfilled in me YOUR purpose, and You've released, in me,
  Your Word.
You merely think a thought about me and then You bring it all to
  birth.
Lord, You've opened heaven's gates and set in motion all my days;
You blew Your breath upon my heart, igniting embers into ablaze.
You've imparted to me—vision, to walk in things unseen;
And then You took me to a depth that far surpassed my greatest
  dreams.
You opened up the book, that my name is written in—
You thumbed through ALL the pages, and showed me where I'd
  been.
Yes, You hold my very life inside the power of Your hands
And You give me Kingdom wisdom and the strength I need to
  stand.
Lord, You've fulfilled in me, Your promises, and called me as Your
  own
You are my future, past AND present—until the day You call me
  home.
You've shown me miracles and wonders and signs from heaven's
  door;
You've tenderized my heart and prepared me, Lord, for MORE!
You've unveiled so many mysteries and things that usually go
  unseen;
You've let me see Through Spirit Eyes—visions, miracles and
  dreams!

My heart is primed and ready to walk in deeper depths unknown
To live in Kingdom Glory, with a life that's Yours alone;
The anointing of Your Spirit, Lord, becomes MORE real to me
  each day;
So, it is with Things Unseen and Awesome Miracles of Faith.

SEPTEMBER 3

KEEPER OF THE LIGHT

A Lighthouse is merely a vessel—
It's just the KEEPER of the Light;
It shines out into the darkness
To the lost who seek to find.
It stands tall in its position—
Its beacon burning bright;
It's like a voice in the distance
Calling out into the night.
It's a promise of a harbor
Safely on the distant shore;
A pinpoint on the horizon
Giving focus in the storm.
It's a shimmering glow of glitter
A beam of shining hope;
It draws the weary traveler
And leads him safely home.
You see, the stately Lighthouse
Is just the KEEPER of the Light;
The REAL treasure of its structure—
Is the LIGHT that burns inside!

SEPTEMBER 4

BEHIND THE WHEEL

My deep desire is to love You, Lord, with all my heart and soul;
To let YOU sit Behind the Wheel and be completely in control.
Not worrying WHERE You'll take me on my journey day to day;
But trusting You in EVERYTHING, in life that comes my way.
For only YOU can know ALL things—where I'm going and where
    I've been;
I merely see the puzzle pieces but You see the beginning and the
    end!
So I need not fear life's journey since You're my compass AND
    my guide;
I relinquish pride's position and I humbly ask You, Lord, to drive!
I trust You, Lord, Behind the Wheel as we travel down life's road;
My journey's safe in Your hands and my life's in Your control.
I know that You are with me and that we're walking side by side
So, Lord, I will go where YOU go and I will trust You with my life.

ONLY IN YOU WILL I MAKE IT

Where are You, Lord, in the battle
When I can't seem to see, feel or hear?
When my heart has been broken and shattered
And all that seem real are my tears?
Lord, why can't I seem to find You
In the suffering and pain of this trial?
It's like the warfare has taken me over
And I've no strength to go the next mile.
How can I face my tomorrows
If you are not with me today;
How can I win in this battle
If I continue in life so afraid?
I need You to help me, Sweet Jesus
For I fear I have lost my way;
Shine Your light and pierce through the darkness
And, Lord, show me YOUR way of escape.
Open the eyes of my heart, Lord
Reveal YOUR purpose and plan;
Fill me with Your Holy Spirit
And guide me with Your outstretched hand.
For Only In You Will I Make It
There's no other way I will win;
So even when I cannot see, feel or hear
By FAITH, Lord, I'll trust in YOUR plan!

SEPTEMBER 6

PEACE WITHIN THE STORM

Human hearts of frailty
Torn apart by pain;
Often search for answers
But often search in vain.
For ONLY Jesus truly knows
Or can come close to understand;
The heartbeat of a person
Or the footsteps of a man.
It's in HIM you must find comfort
When you feel pulled apart and torn;
It's the peace that Jesus gives
When you're shattered by the storm.
And when heartache and confusion
Appear so valid and extreme;
You must look to HIM for answers
So, HIS answers can be seen.
He understands the frailty
Inside the heart of man;
And when you run to Him for comfort
He'll give the GRACE you need to stand.
So in the midst of pain that pierces
To the depth of one's own soul;
May peace be found in Jesus
And love that He bestows.
For only HE can truly give
Peace Within the Storm;
And only HE can calm the winds
And give you strength to carry on.

THE MOUTH OF THE LION HAS OPENED AND HE'S RELEASING A MIGHTY ROAR

A host of angelic warriors are released and ready for war;
The Mouth of the Lion Has Opened—and He's Releasing a
   Mighty Roar!
Masses of heavenly creatures, too many for man's eyes to see;
Invading the enemy's darkness, and changing man's destiny.
Swift is the sword they carry, as they ride on the breath of the
   wind;
They are conquering angels of judgment, sent on behalf of men.
If only our eyes could witness what happens in the realm we can't
   see;
We'd know that He's piercing the darkness, and He's winning the
   victory!
Yes, a host of angelic warriors are released and ready for war;
The Mouth of the Lion Has Opened—and He's Releasing a
   Mighty Roar!

SEPTEMBER 8

A BEAM OF HEAVEN'S GLORY

A burst of heaven's sunlight
Piercing through the clouds of gray;
Riding on the wings of Glory,
Unveiling hope in dark-filled days.
Whispering, God's sweet presence,
Upon the landscape's wall;
Like a portrait on a canvas
That draws men's hearts to God!
A place where hope's transparent
And put upon display;
As God stretches forth His finger
And points direction for the way.
Like a lighthouse in the distance
Or a shimmer in the night;
Revealing Love's Sweet Promise
That everything will be all right.
Giving breakthrough for the morning
Through God's celestial ray;
It's a Beam of Heaven's Glory—
Releasing HOPE to guide the way!

SEPTEMBER 9

THE RACE IS ALMOST OVER

The winds of war are blowing,
Across the raging sea;
The trumpeteer's NOW standing
And we are SOON, to Hear and See!
Yes, the end, as we all know it,
Is so very close at hand;
The breath of God is breathing,
And it's covering our land!
The race that we are running
Has reached its FINAL lap;
The finish line's before us,
And we can see the end at last!
So, remember, Don't Give Up
For the battle's ALMOST won;
And we WILL see the lights of Glory
When it's all been said and done.
Fear Not, within the struggle,
Instead, be disciplined in stride;
For the Race Is Almost Over
And SOON, We'll Cross the Finish Line!

SEPTEMBER 10

SWEET LORD

Through every trial, I seem to find, my way to You, Sweet Lord;
Seeking refuge in Your safety, and PEACE, inside the storm!
Seems so funny, how the battles, which were meant to kill and
    steal;
Only draw me to my knees in prayer, and into YOUR perfect will.
It's almost like a looking glass, to reflect on WHERE I am;
Completely, Lord, dependent—upon Your loving hand!
So, when I'm in the battle, feeling weary, tired and worn;
I'll look to find the open path—that leads to YOU, Sweet Lord!

SEPTEMBER 11

TO BEHOLD THE LIGHT OF YOUR FACE

Entering in, to the fullness of life—
An inheritance promised by You;
An abundance of rain and the taste of new wine
As I come to the Light of Your Truth.
I will be glad and rejoice in You, Lord,
As Your favor falls like the dew;
I will shout with the voice of victory
And keep my eyes and my heart upon You.
With unlimited access I'll enter in,
Where Your presence is all that I breathe;
Consumed in the fullness of heaven's caress
Carried high upon angels' wings.
My celebration comes in the light of Your face
For in the light of Your face there is life;
I will function today in Your covering grace
As I stand in Your marvelous light.
I will come with a confident spirit
And receive Your abundance of rain;
With boldness, I'll bow in Your presence—
And I'll Behold the Light of your Face!

WINGS OF A DOVE

Lord, grant me the courage and the strength I will need;
To continue life's race and YOUR purpose for me.
Help me NOT to lose faith by what I see with my eyes;
Instead cause it to grow, bestowing grace to my life;
For Your ways aren't my ways, they're much higher than mine;
So, when my hope is deferred, speak peace to my mind.
And when the trials and struggles seem too heavy a load;
Lift the weight from my shoulders, onto Your own.
Give me wisdom to know that, You, are STILL in control;
In the midst of the battle , where the crisp cold winds blow.
Enlighten my heart, Lord, so my eyes can see;
New hope for tomorrow and YOUR love for me.
Send Your Sweet Holy Presence on the Wings of a Dove;
Capture ALL of me, Lord, and surround me with love!

CLINGING TO THE CROSS

I'm tired of life's struggles, and heartfelt despair;
But, I'm grateful to God, to meet me there.
In the depth of the tomb, He lifts me up;
He breathes in His breath, and I rise above!
I Cling to the Cross and I fall at His feet;
My soul is encouraged, and my heart skips a beat!
The darkness around me ceases to be;
As the light of the Lord, shines down on me!
His Glory is GREAT and His Mercy is New;
In the depth of the pit, He restores and renews!
So, I Cling to the Cross, in the midst of despair;
And I lift up to God on the wings of a prayer!
There is no place on earth, that can keep me from Him;
Nor darkness to cover HIS light within!
I Cling to the Cross, His Oasis of Love;
He breathes in His breath—and I rise above!

SEPTEMBER 14

SHELTER IN THE STORM

When I cry unto You, Lord, I know that You'll be there;
And when my heart is breaking, I'll be confident, You care!
When my mind's comprehension becomes blurred by flowing
    tears;
I'll know that You're STILL listening, and calming all my fears!
For, Father, You have promised, that You would NEVER leave me;
Instead, You put Your mark upon me, and it's YOU, who has
    redeemed me!
So, when the struggles that I'm facing, try to steal my faith away;
I'll keep my focus upon YOU—I refuse to lose my way!
I know You're MORE than able, to help me rise above;
Every circumstance of life, that the devil could dream up!
So, I'll rest within Your shadow, when I'm weary and forlorn;
And I'll run into YOUR arms, where I'll find Shelter in the Storm!

HIS KISS UPON MY FACE

I cannot catch the blowing wind—
Still, I know, it's there;
I cannot see it with my eyes
But I can FEEL it in the air.
It's like heaven's doorway opens
And God breathes His breath of life;
My soul awakens from the depths
And it leaps to greater heights.
His lovely fragrance covers me
With the smell of sweet perfume;
And the veil that once did cover
Has now been lifted and removed!
Yes, the passion of His mighty love
Envelopes who I am;
He captures me to be His Own
And holds me safely in His hand.
So, today, I am reminded
Of where the wind does blow;
As I keep a watch upon my heart
And His majesty behold.
I lift my face to heaven's door
And breathe in His embrace;
As He blows His breath upon me
And puts His Kiss upon My Face!

September 16

Apple of God's Eye

God looked across creation
And saw His handiwork displayed;
The earth in all its beauty
And the heavens He had made.
But even all He gazed upon
Could not compare with you;
For He formed and made you special
With His kiss of morning dew.
He touched you with His tenderness
And His ability to love
He covered you with grace
And sprinkled blessings from above.
All of those who know you
Have been touched by God's own hand;
You've made a difference to so many
Time and time again.
Yes, you're the Father's handiwork
A valued treasure in this life;
You are a blessing sent from heaven
You're the Apple of God's Eye.

SEPTEMBER 17

UPON THE POTTER'S WHEEL

The potter's hand is always moving
To shape the clay with constant love;
The potter's hand is fast removing
All debris of grit and scum.
Caressed by steadfast thoughts
To form and shape a piece of clay;
From an ugly lump of mud
Into an image HE creates.
The time it takes the potter
Portrays His heart within;
To design and mold a vessel
From beginning to the end.
The clay becomes the image
Fashioned by the potter's hands;
Shaped and molded for a purpose
And a most specific Plan.
Transformation of the vessel
And beauty that it yields;
Is created by the Master
Upon the Potter's Wheel!

FOOTSTOOL OF THE THRONE

Lightening streaks across the sky
And mighty thunders roll;
From the height of heaven's doorway
His awesome majesty unfolds.
Beyond man's eyes are wonders
Too exquisite to behold;
Inside His realm of Glory;
At the Footstool of the Throne.
A place where secrets rendered
Become like sweet perfume;
Nestled in His bosom
Within a mercy that consumes.
It's a place where every mystery
Never ceases to unfold;
Where light exposes darkness
And His wondrous works explode.
It's a place where all created
Give honor to the King;
Unbridled in their passion
To worship at His feet.
Yes, Inside His Realm of Glory—
At the Footstool of the Throne;
His love does far exceed
More than man could dare behold.

PURIFIED GOLD

The bigger the problem—the "BIGGER" my God;
For, it's WHEN I am weak, He makes me strong!
It's the fires I face, in my life EVERY day;
That cause me to grow, and teach me, to pray!
You see, there's nothing too big, that God cannot do;
And with Him on my side, I can do ALL things, TOO!
He's perfecting the details, in every part of my life;
He's conforming me DAILY, to be MORE like Christ!
So, when I FEEL fire, and the heat from its glow;
I'll know, I'm in PROCESS—of becoming pure Gold!

MY LIFE IS BUT A JOURNEY

Lord, I cannot SEE Your face nor always HEAR the words You
    speak;
But, I'm a witness of Your power, that often brings me to Your
    feet.
I cannot fully understand the greatness You display
But, I'm a walking testimony, of Your never-ending grace.
My heart can't always fathom, exactly ALL You have for me;
For sometimes, I find I question, what You've raised me up to be.
But it doesn't really matter if I know all the ends and outs;
For, my heart's joy is to obey You, with a faith that doesn't doubt.
So, I'll bring my purpose and my destiny, and I'll lay them at Your
    feet;
And I will trust YOU in the process, until my life becomes
    complete.
Lord, I pray that when it's hard, I will not sink upon the sand;
Instead, I'll yield my heart to You, and live according to Your plan.
For My Life Is but a Journey that leads me to Your throne;
My destination is in YOU, Lord, and my heart belongs to YOU,
    alone!

THE TREASURE HIS
HEART HOLDS

Standing on the shoreline, I heard the thunder roar
So majestic in the distance but yet I knew it was the Lord.
My heart began to ponder my significance to Him
And I realized how He talks to me time and time again.
Whether high upon the mountain's peak or in the valley low;
I Find I'm His Beloved—I'm the Treasure His Heart Holds.
For there is no height too high to reach, nor depth He will not go;
And never will I find myself, afraid to be alone.
My heart is His forever and I am always in His care;
There will never be a moment's time when He will not be there.
For He knows when I am sleeping, He knows when I awake;
He even knows ahead of time, every choice I'll ever make.
He's never caught off guard by what I say or do;
And when I miss the mark, He's always there to pull me through.
He picks me up when I am down and dries my every tear
He wipes away the heartache and whispers love songs in my ear.
He has given me His presence like a kiss upon my soul
Without a doubt, I'm His Beloved—I'm the Treasure His Heart
    Holds!

SEASON OF YOUR GRACE

The smell of Your sweet fragrance drifts in upon the breeze
And I can sense Your lovely presence in the very air I breathe.
I can hear the sound of heaven rumbling softly in my ear
And I can see Your light of glory embracing all that's near.
My heart shall dance in victory for this time of Jubilee;
For I have witnessed Heaven's Glory—I receive it and believe.
Lord, I can feel Your gentle rain as it falls upon my face
As I'm standing in Your presence—in this Season of Your Grace.

MY SONG TO HIM

I heard a songbird sing today
With a melody so sweet;
And as I listened most intently—
I heard my Father speak.
He told me of His love for me
Through this simple little song
He stirred my spirit deep within;
And sent His message loud and strong.
For He loves the tiny sparrow
And the praise HE humbly gives;
So, How much MORE will He love ME
When I sing MY Song—to Him?

POLISHED GEM

Tossed about by circumstance and confused along the way;
Hindered by the things I SEE, and the grief of each new day.
Afraid to face tomorrow, in the fear that I might fail;
Discouraged in the battle—wounded, tired and frail.
But, no matter WHAT the circumstance or grief that comes my
    way;
By FAITH, I'll stand in Jesus, even when I FEEL afraid!
For, I know that He'll deliver, when I patiently await;
Cause I'm a Gem That's Being Polished, through the friction, He,
    creates!
I'll come through each adversity, with a sparkle and a gleam;
For the Master's hand is polishing, and He won't stop, until I'm
    clean!

SEPTEMBER 25

LIFE'S NOT PERFECT

If everything was easy, in this life that I go through;
And if everything were perfect, I'd probably have no need for
 You!
But, it's the trials in my life, that bring me to my knees;
They remind me, I am helpless, I am human, frail and weak!
I find I cannot stand, OUTSIDE Your perfect Grace;
For, it's Your love that gets me through, every rough and rocky
 place!
It's the scars of every trial, that continue to remind;
I need You every day, in my life, to stay alive!
So, Lord, I'd rather have life's struggles and all that I go through;
Than a perfect life, ALONE—where I would have NO need for
 You!

September 26

Send Your Love

You are my strength when I have none
You are the hope in the race I run;
Yes, You, Oh Lord, are ALL I need
My faith's in You, You are ALL to me!
So when I find myself afraid
Speak peace within and calm each wave;
Lord, Send Your Love on angels' wings
And raise me up AGAIN to sing!

September 27

Kingdom Vision

May I NOT see through colored glasses
Nor live my life in compromise;
Instead, I pray for Kingdom Vision—
So I can see things through YOUR eyes.
I ask for Your discernment
Greater than I've known before;
That my focus would be sharp
And set upon YOU, Lord!
May I rise up in the Spirit
And perceive with Godly eyes;
Clear vision for the Kingdom
And YOUR purpose for my life.
Loose me from captivity
And this dark night of my soul;
Give me—Kingdom Vision, Lord
And YOUR wonders to behold.

SEPTEMBER 28

WINGS OF PRAYER

My grief's beyond healing, and my heart is found broken;
My eyes can't stop weeping, and words can't be spoken!
The sound of the silence, shatters my peace;
And the screams of my soul, seem to find no release!
Where are You, Lord, in the midst of this grief;
Can You feel what I feel—do Your ears hear me weep?
Do the tears that flow down, and drop from my face;
Find a place in Your presence, covered by Grace?
Where is the kiss of the morning dew;
That bids me to "COME", and fall before You?
In that place that's reserved for Your children to be;
Where hope becomes LIFE, on the inside of me.
A refuge of safety, in that place where YOU dwell;
Where nothing else matters, but the TRUTH that prevails!
Call me to come, Lord, and I will be there;
I will soar like an eagle, on the wings of a prayer!
Inside YOUR presence, may this broken heart find;
Peace for the journey and strength of the climb!

SEPTEMBER 29

THE BEAUTY OF HIS MASTERPIECE

I now see through the glass so dimly
Because I can't comprehend it all;
For it seems too complex for my mind
To grasp the full concept of God.
It's as if I look through a window
And stained glass is all I can see;
Only shards and broken pieces of color
A detailed puzzle just made complete.
I can't help but be amazed
At each lovely and beautiful piece;
How each one fits with another
To create such a masterpiece.
Well, MY life is like the stained glass
Broken pieces fit together as one;
Each the depth and the color of triumph—
Mere symbols of past victories won.
You see, My heart knows when my life is over
When summer has turned into fall;
I'll walk in the glory of my Jesus
And I'll have the full knowledge of God.
For HIS light will become the reflection
That illuminates EACH piece in me;
And every part of me that was broken
Will become the Beauty of HIS Masterpiece!

THE SEASONS OF A LIFE

Seasons are distinct and they will never cease,
Whether seed or harvest time, cold or summer's heat.
Well, also, life's a series that follows certain ways;
There's no pattern to the process that every season takes.
For the Father has a purpose and specifics to fulfill
And oftentimes there's waiting until it's all revealed.
There's always work involved and something to be done.
Whether in the cold of winter or the heat of summer's sun.
Yes, God will put us in a season but the time will NOT be lost,
For everything that happens is covered by the plan of God.

God's Whisper in the Breeze
Until the Morning Breaks
I Know You'll Be There
Dark Night of My Soul
The Weight of Every Burden
Vision of the Gardener
My Destiny Is Jesus
Your Promises Are Sure
Patiently Waiting
Faithful Word
My Life's in His Hands
Extra Mile
God of Second Chances
Ever Faithful Promise
Follow My Lead—Walk Where I Walk
Always on Time
The Latter Rain
Only God Can Heal
He's My Provision
Measure of Faith
He's My Joy in Life's Journey
Standing in the Glow of God's Glory
Walking by Your Side
Safe Within God's Dwelling Place
My Story's God's Glory
Competence of Character
Shadow of the Lord
Glory's Home Is Eternal
I'll Rest Within the Peace of God
God's Setting Sun
Once Again We'll Fly

OCTOBER 1

GOD'S WHISPER IN THE BREEZE

Are you focused on God's Whisper, as It Rides upon the Breeze;
Have you heard His tender calling, within the blowing leaves?
If you will take the time to listen, with ears tuned in to hear;
You'll find that His Sweet Spirit, is always there to draw you near!
For, it's only in the solitude, shut away from earthly things;
That you will truly hear God's voice, in the song the sparrow
     sings.
He will strum your heart so gently, by the very breath He
     breathes;
And you'll be swept away in Glory—safe beneath His
     outstretched wings!
Yes, it's only in His shadow, that CALM will ride with ease;
Upon the dawn's sweet solace, atop the windswept trees!
To a place where only peace, can soothe your ravaged soul;
Where life takes on new meaning and HOPE becomes your hold.
So, take some time and ponder, the rustling of the leaves,
Because you, MIGHT, just hear God's Whisper—
As It Rides upon the Breeze!

OCTOBER 2

UNTIL THE MORNING BREAKS

If I can only wait 'til morning, when the light of dawn breaks
    through;
Then maybe I'll have strength—to focus, Lord, on YOU!
For it's in the night's dark hours, that the warfare takes its toll;
When I'm lost inside the shadows and I've no more self-control.
It's where agony, meets torment, and drags me in to play;
Where I'm left to fight the battles, with no light to guide my way.
I cry out, "Abba Father," but my eyes just cannot see;
For the darkness closes in and wraps its ugly arms round me.
My heart is bound by fetters and chains constrict my soul;
My vision is distorted and I don't know which way to go.
I am looking for the sunlight to burst upon the scene
To break the ties that bind, this all-consuming dream.
I am praying for the hand of God, to reach through time and
    space
And deliver me in victory from this dark and cruel place.
I will look for joy's promise to ride in upon the breeze
To usher in the dawn of day and speak God's sweet release.
Yes, I'll hold on until the Morning—where the light of dawn
    breaks through
In that place where only YOU, Lord, can comfort, heal and
    soothe.
My heart yields to the HOPE—that when darkness seeks to hold,
You will emerge with wings of healing and blow Your breath
    upon my soul!

OCTOBER 3

I KNOW YOU'LL BE THERE

Lord, today I come before You
Exhausted from the load;
My vision has been clouded
And I don't know which way to go.
I am searching for Your presence
I am looking for Your light;
I need You, Lord, to guide me
Through this season of my life.
I'm like a ship upon the water
Lost inside a storm;
The winds are fiercely blowing
And I am battered, tired and torn!
I ask, Oh Lord, that You alone
Would calm the raging sea;
That You would walk upon the water—
That You would come and rescue me.
I know that You will save me
From the dark tides of despair;
For when I call upon Your Name,
Lord, I Know That You'll Be There.

OCTOBER 4

DARK NIGHT OF MY SOUL

I find myself in darkness in spite of where I've been;
The light that used to guide me is now faded, gray and dim.
I'm desperate to find Jesus, for with Him, I know I'm whole;
But I'm lost inside the shadows—in this Dark Night of My Soul.
I cannot seem to find my way nor escape this pit I'm in;
I'm estranged from all the comforts and all I've ever known of
    Him.
My heart's fire is but an ember that has dwindled to a glow;
As I struggle to find my way through this Dark Night of My Soul.
As I wait for my beloved and His presence once again;
I must keep His love—my focus, Even when the light grows dim.
For He is looking for maturity, in me, His lovely Bride;
I'm not alone inside the darkness nor am I lost from Jesus' eyes.
Even in the midst of shadows—in this Dark Night of My Soul;
My heart DOES hold the promise, that my God's STILL in
    control

THE WEIGHT OF EVERY BURDEN

Will the weight of my burdens become the wings that help me fly;
Will the load upon my shoulder, actually aim me toward the sky?
As I lift my troubles upward, my heart begins to soar;
They become my very airlift, in which I rise to meet the Lord.
When I cheerfully bear a burden, knowing God is always there;
It becomes a lovely blessing, instead of deep despair.
I won't refuse to bend my shoulders, to receive the burden of a
    load;
For the weight that I will carry, becomes my opportunity to grow.
I only need remember, that the weight my shoulders bear;
Brings me closer to the Father, when I bow my heart in prayer.
I know the weight the burden brings, will become the wings that
    help me fly;
For it's the load upon my shoulders, that lifts my heart toward
    heaven's sky!

OCTOBER 6
VISION OF THE GARDENER

The gardener looks upon his garden
And knows the branches MUST be pruned;
So he cuts and trims severely,
And gets them READY to bear fruit.
For a luscious crop is being grown
With fruit that's perfect, plump and sweet;
But it can't come to fruition,
Until the pruning is complete.
The unpruned branch will just LOOK good,
But it's fruit is hard to find;
Because it's shriveled up and bitter,
And hangs lifeless, on the vine.
The Vision of the Gardener
Is to see the garden yield its BEST;
So, he prunes away the excess,
And nurtures carefully the rest.
The gardener's eyes are ALWAYS focused
On what the "harvest day" will bring;
So, he attends the garden faithfully,
Until ALL the work's complete.

OCTOBER 7

MY DESTINY IS JESUS

I have climbed the rocky mountain
I have scaled its steepest wall;
Even when it wasn't easy
And I thought I'd surely fall.
But , no matter how discouraged,
I continued in the climb;
It's like my faith propelled me higher
Than the doubts that plagued my mind.
I believe that unseen angels
Were dispersed to carry me;
As I struggled up the mountain
Toward my promised destiny
You see, my journey takes me upward
To the foot of heaven's throne;
And so, I cannot lose my vision
Nor allow my thoughts to roam.
Today, I'm just a pilgrim
Traveling through a foreign land;
But My Destiny Is JESUS
And He will always hold my hand.
So, I'll continue this life's journey
And climb the mountain wall;
I will keep my focus, steady—
Knowing, HE, won't let me fall!

OCTOBER 8

YOUR PROMISES ARE SURE

I've stumbled over mountaintops
I've been through valleys low;
I've struggled in the darkness
Yet, I've managed to behold—
That You are ALWAYS with me
No matter where I am;
You're the anchor that holds my heart
In alignment with Your plan.
There is never any place I'll be
Outside Your loving reach;
Whether on the mountaintop
Or the ocean floor so deep.
Father, You are ALWAYS there—
You're the Light that guides my way;
You keep me safe in storms
And calm my fears when I'm afraid.
I know You'll never leave me—
Yes, Your Promises Are Sure;
No matter where You lead me
In YOU, I'll STAY Secure.

OCTOBER 9

PATIENTLY WAITING

Lord, I know You're in control
No matter WHAT I see;
You're aware of every circumstance,
That rears its ugly head at me.
I may not NOW perceive Your will,
Nor comprehend Your plan;
But I'm learning, Lord, to trust You,
In the midst of WHERE I am.
I know that You will lift me
From this pit of deep despair;
And set my feet on solid ground
Even when life seems unfair.
For I know that when I call to You—
You will hear my every plea;
Because You're a God that NEVER slumbers
And You're intently watching me.
So, I pray that I'll be patient,
And wait upon YOUR will;
Trusting, You, for EVERY answer
No matter how, I FEEL!

OCTOBER 10

FAITHFUL WORD

(Inspired by Psalm 119:92–95)

Though the wicked are ruthless
And hide along the way;
To destroy and kill
And make me afraid.
I will quietly keep
My mind on Your Word;
On every promise You've made
And truth that I've heard.
I would have truly despaired
And perished by night;
If Your laws had not been
My deepest delight;
I am Yours and I trust You
To restore and make new;
Even when I feel shattered
Broken and bruised.

OCTOBER 11
My Life's in His Hands

On the brink of the ages
I patiently wait;
Holding firm to each promise
My Savior has made.
And no matter what happens—
His plan WILL unfold;
It will be just as He said
By the prophets of old.
For He knew long ago
World events would arise;
He's not caught unaware
Nor is He surprised.
But in the midst of it all
He is STILL in control;
He knows every detail
Of what future days hold.
So my peace is in knowing
That in Him I'm secure;
Even when the earth shakes
And everything's so unsure.
For there's nothing on earth
That can keep me from Him;
Neither darkness or famine
Or the world's very end.
My faith is in Jesus
And THAT'S where I'll stand;
You see, my journey's in Him
And MY LIFE'S IN HIS HANDS.

OCTOBER 12

EXTRA MILE

My heart knows not the answers
Of daily struggles that I face;
But it knows the strength within me
As I FEEL Your warm embrace.
You see, I may not always understand
Every THING that I go through;
But it really doesn't matter
As long as I go through them, Lord, with YOU!
So, when I find myself in strife
And overcome by earthly trials;
Please encourage me to "run the race"—
And go that Extra Mile!

God of Second Chances

You must rest assured on promises,
Given by the Lord;
No matter WHAT, you're facing,
Keep your eyes on the reward.
Yes, God WILL bring deliverance,
He will not let you fail;
So, stay faithful to His Word—
Until HIS truth, prevails.
You must never make provision
To go back to where you were;
You must never entertain a lie
Nor compromise your worth.
There is nothing in this world
More valuable than YOU;
So. keep purity within,
No matter WHAT, you're going through.
For the battle always shows
Where you walk from day to day;
You're either living in His Glory—
Or in the depth of deep heartache.
But once you've had a taste.
Of the Father's precious love;
You'll know, HE has the answers,
And HIS peace, WILL BE—ENOUGH.
Yes, He's a God of Second Chances,
And His promises are true;
His covenant's FOREVER
And He's ALWAYS there for you!

OCTOBER 14

EVER FAITHFUL PROMISE

Lord, You are my Alpha and Omega
My Beginning and my End;
You are more than just the one I love,
You walk beside me hand in hand.
Yes, everyday grows sweeter
Upon my journey's road;
And my heart is much more confident
For I no longer walk alone.
So, no matter where life takes me
I know that You'll be there;
Ever Faithful in Your Promise
To keep me safe within Your care.

Follow My Lead— Walk Where I Walk

Step where I step, follow Me child;
Walk where I walk, trust Me awhile.
Focus your heart and your eyes upon Me;
Enjoy the climb and stay close to My lead.
There's no need to fear that you'll stumble or fall;
When you follow My footsteps up the mountain's steep wall;
The lesson is simple, merely learn to depend;
And I'll take you higher than you've ever been.
Trust Me to guide you to the summit's lush top;
Just step where I step and walk where I walk.
Place your feet in My footprints and your life in My hands;
And when the journey's complete—you'll be where I am.
Continue to climb, never look back or stop;
Just Follow My Lead and Walk Where I Walk!

OCTOBER 16

ALWAYS ON TIME

Not once has God failed, to show up on time;
To bring answers to prayer, and give peace to my mind.
For in the midst of the problem, He was ALWAYS aware;
Of every burden I carried and each heartache I'd bear.
And at just the right moment, He'd intercede and come through;
He never once was too late, nor was He ever too soon.
He was ALWAYS on Time, He was NEVER caught by surprise;
You see, His perspective on things, is so much clearer than mine.
For I'd worry and squirm, and do battle within;
While my mind, in doubt, wondered, if I'd survive to the end.
But no matter what happened, He stayed faithful to me;
Each promise He made, He was consistent to keep.
So, I'll try hard to remember, when I don't see a sign;
That God is STILL in control, and He is Always on Time!

OCTOBER 17

THE LATTER RAIN

Is our trust upon the mammon, that controls this mighty land;
Or upon the God of Righteousness—who IS the Great I Am?
For IF we seek, just merely substance, instead of trusting HIM;
We'll miss His Mighty Blessings and the gifts that He will give!
You see, this is a time of testing—to find where TRUE allegiance
    lies;
Are we more concerned with money, OR, the outcome of our
    lives?
The line's now being drawn, upon the dusty shore;
We hold within, the balance, choosing "Man's Way's"—OR "The
    Lord's!"
What IS the most important when it's all been said and done;
Will we choose the God of mammon, or the Righteous Holy
    One?
So, before we make decisions based upon the things we SEE;
May we take the time to bow our hearts and to fall upon our
    knees!
For God is looking for a people, that will put their trust in HIM;
Who will not fold to compromise nor sell their souls to sin.
A people that will WAIT—until HIS Spirit moves;
And NOT give up the battle, nor turn away from truth.
It's when things seem uncertain, that we MUST call upon His
    Name;
For, He has promised, in due season, He would send the Latter
    Rain!

OCTOBER 18

ONLY GOD CAN HEAL

Time only dulls the memories and the sting of bitter pain;
It cannot take away the hurt or erase its ugly stain.
Forever etched upon the heart, are tattered scars left there by
time;
Now faded memories, in the distance, and hurtful heartache left
behind.
Some people say that time will heal those wounds that pierce so
deep;
But how can they access the pain of a heart that's full of grief.
Seems the tears just stream unceasingly and the eyes can't help
but cry;
For it's so hard to fully understand as one seeks to
reason—WHY?
Time will NEVER be the answer, to heal the brokenness within;
You see, time can NEVER heal a heart nor does it have the ability
to mend.
Only Jesus truly understands , the depths of heartache's sting;
Because He also suffered cruelty and the devastation that it
brings.
The Lord now holds the answer to those who felt as if they've
died;
He has compassion for the hurting, and the pain they feel inside.
His desire is to heal, He wants to comfort and restore;
For only He can soothe a savage heart and calm the raging storm.

OCTOBER 19

HE'S MY PROVISION

He's My Provision, because that's, WHO He is;
He supplies all my needs, to live triumphant in Him;
You see, HE brings to pass, ALL things in my life;
HIS Grace is sufficient, and His promises—MINE!
When, in Him, I abide, His Word lives in me;
He opens the heavens and allows me to see.
That, MY God, is a BIG God, who can do ANY thing;
He brings me through trials and gives a NEW song to sing!
For MY God delights, in a heart turned to Him;
He opens His arms and He welcomes me in.
So, because He is with me, I'll stand and fear not;
I will put on HIS armor and I WILL trust in My God!
Yes, He's My Provision, because I'M in the vine;
His truth is my hope, and His promises—MINE!

OCTOBER 20

MEASURE OF FAITH

My faith is the measure by which I believe,
it's the ultimate test in my life;
It's the position I take when I'm trusting in God
for the strength to continue the fight.
It's the hope in my heart that carries me through,
when my eyes cannot see past the storm;
It's the peace from God's throne that rises within
and gently whispers for me to go on.
It's the grace of God's touch in the midst of the trial
to calm and reveal His sweet love;
To know that no matter WHAT I go through, in my life—
He is ALWAYS enough!
Like a torch raised up in the battle,
it chases the darkness away;
For when I am weak, I find I am strong—
and in Him, I'm no longer afraid.
Yes, my faith is the measure by which I believe,
it's truly my ultimate stand;
It's my banner waved high on the landscape of life,
it's a portrait of ALL that I am!

OCTOBER 21

HE'S MY JOY IN LIFE'S JOURNEY

My life is blessed with joy
And Jesus IS its source;
For the indwelling of His Spirit
Releases HIS joy to pour forth.
My vision NOW is higher
I see myself through His own eyes;
You see, He doesn't see my every flaw—
He only sees—a lovely bride!
His joy's the ignition
That sets my feet on Holy Ground;
It causes me to dwell within
His supernatural realm.
His joy IS in my life—
In Him I'm most complete;
No matter what the circumstance
I will NOT face defeat!
For He is ALWAYS with me
My heart belongs to Him;
He's My Joy in Life's Journey—
He's the reason that I live!

STANDING IN THE GLOW
OF GOD'S GLORY

To stand in the glow of God's glory,
as dry bones rattle and take on new life;
To rise from the ashes of death and defeat,
to life with our risen Christ.
Allowing the Spirit of Jesus, Himself,
to breathe life where death had its hold;
To raise up an army to march in the land,
causing miraculous signs to unfold.
His anointing will cover the nameless,
and the faceless one's whom He'll choose;
Those who DON'T seek self-promotion,
but are submitted for God to use.
God, Himself, will blow a loud trumpet,
that will call all men to the light;
He will establish His Kingdom on earth,
and darkness will flee in the night.
The Lord will arise over each one He calls,
and His Glory will be seen by them all;
His brightness will shine like the dawn's early light,
and the focus will be ONLY on God.
The least will become a thousand,
and the smallest a nation so great;
For the Lord is preparing HIS army,
and determining the enemy's fate.
The work of God's Kingdom is hastened,
and the clouds of His Glory descend;
The spout is tipped for the pouring,
for a NEW work He plans to begin.
It's time to step boldly into God's will,
and receive ALL the portion assigned;
To enter into the very presence of God,
and let HIM raise the dry bones to life!

October 23

Walking by Your Side

Never look with fear and doubt,
But with heartfelt anticipation;
At ALL the Lord can do,
In the midst of devastation.
For NOTHING shakes His confidence
Nor catches Him off guard;
He's well aware of EVERYTHING,
Right from the very start!
So, be strong, my friend, with courage,
And trust the Lord to guide;
For He is ever watching,
And Walking by Your Side!

OCTOBER 24

SAFE WITHIN GOD'S DWELLING PLACE

(Read Psalm 91)

I'm Safe Within God's Dwelling Place—
The shelter of His love;
He's my refuge and my fortress—
My God, in whom I trust.
He saves me from the fowler's snare
And every plague designed to kill;
He covers me with feathers—
I am safe within His Will.
I stand within God's faithfulness
Shielded in this life;
I will not fear the arrows
Nor the terror of the night.
Though death may fall in darkness
My life's secure, it's true;
For my dwelling place is found
Within HIS safety and refuge!
No evil will befall me
Nor bring harm to me this day;
For my God commissions angels
To watch over all my ways.
I am Safe Within God's Dwelling Place—
The shelter of His love;
He's my refuge and my fortress—
My God, in whom I trust!

OCTOBER 25

MY STORY'S GOD'S GLORY

My faith will often lead me—to the wilderness, forlorn;
But no matter WHERE I'm led, I'll keep my eyes upon the Lord.
You see, regardless of my turmoil, my faith's sustained in Him;
And IF, I'll stand and wait, He WILL deliver me to WIN!
So, in my tribulation, I will glorify the King;
I will put my trust in knowing, that ,He's aware of
    EVERYTHING!
He knows me on the mountain but also in the valley low;
He pours His strength within me and sustains my heavy load.
So, I'll use my faith to lead me, into a closer walk with Him;
Where victory is His promise and deliverance is His plan.
Yes, MY Story Is God's Glory, so I will testify to you;
Of all that He has done for me, and all He's brought me through!

COMPETENCE OF CHARACTER

Qualify me Jesus
Make me adequate I pray;
Demonstrate Your power
Through my yieldedness today.
May You find me always faithful—
In ALL I say and do;
And may my heart be truly focused
Only upon YOU!
Lord, pour forth Your anointing
And give me eyes to clearly see;
Vision for Your Kingdom
And what You're equipping me to be.
May I function in Your body
Not overlooking little things;
But giving notice to every detail
And the importance each one brings.
Give me Competence of Character
And great exploits to fulfill;
Bring my life into alignment
That I might live to do Your Will.

OCTOBER 27

SHADOW OF THE LORD

Lord, lift me from the miry clay
And the pit that pulls me down;
Rescue me, today, I pray,
And set my feet on solid ground!
Place Your hope within my heart
And give me eyes to see;
Deliverance through Your Spirit,
Against my EVERY enemy!
Restore to me, some peace of mind,
And lead me through the day;
Walk with me, and cover me,
Beneath Your Shadow, Lord, I pray!

OCTOBER 28

GLORY'S HOME IS ETERNAL

I Was Made to Last Forever and death will NOT have a hold;
For, NOW, is but a moment, but one day I'll be home.
This world will surely fade away like a breath upon a wind;
Preparing me for greater heights than I have ever been.
I am wired for eternity, I was not designed to roam;
I'm headed for a destination where heaven is my home.
One day God will call me there beyond the life that I now see;
And I will set my foot in Glory and I'll behold eternity.
You see, death will never terminate or end the life of man;
For it is only the beginning in God's eternal plan.
I am but a pilgrim—a blink within an eye;
And One day life will end and my natural body die.
It's then that I will understand that death brings only birth;
And I will stand and give account of how I lived my life on earth.
So while I'm here, I WILL prepare, for this world is not my home;
I will keep my eyes on Jesus until I stand before His throne.
Yes, I Was Made to Last Forever in the presence of the Lord;
Where Glory's Home's Eternal and Jesus Is the Door!

OCTOBER 29

I'LL REST WITHIN THE PEACE OF GOD

Anxiety becomes a mighty tool
Within the devil's hands;
It magnifies my problems
And makes it hard for me to stand.
So I must NOT open up that door
Which allows fear to enter in;
Instead, I'll trust in Jesus
And cast ALL my cares on Him!
I WILL hold tightly to the truth
And cling ALWAYS to the Lord;
Even when I'm tired and weary—
I'll keep my hand upon God's sword.
For He has given me assignment
He didn't call me to retreat;
He placed His hand upon me
And laid HIS path before my feet.
So, I will recognize anxiety
As warfare to be fought;
And through prayer and supplication,
I'll Rest Within—the Peace of God!

OCTOBER 30

GOD'S SETTING SUN

Across the plains, we see,
The sun make its way;
Past the landscape of life,
Before fading away.
And then once it's gone,
Colors are left to portray;
The contrast of beauty
That was created that day.
I'm not really sure
That justice is done;
When one tries to describe
God's Setting Sun.
For, it's His special goodnight
As He turns off the light;
Leaving the stars and the moon
To shine through the night.
God's sunset's consistent—
It's His own special way;
To show His love for the world
At the end of the day!

OCTOBER 31

ONCE AGAIN WE'LL FLY

Soaring high above the trees, far from obstacles below;
I saw a tiny sparrow, with lovely beauty to behold!
I saw him make it through the storm, and winds along his way;
Yet, safely land atop a tree, that was briskly being swayed.
He was battered by the tossing wind and the harshness of its
    blow;
But, no matter WHAT the circumstance, he never was alone!
For, God's eye was ON the sparrow and there was shelter for the
    bird;
He may seem insignificant but, to God, he has great worth!
So, if the Lord, watches o'er the sparrow, as it takes its wings to
    fly;
How much MORE concerned, is He, with what faces you and I?
I believe that God delivers and gives shelter from each storm;
That, His eye, is ever watching when we're weary, tired and worn!
And when the winds are over and the storms have passed us by;
We, too, are like the sparrow—and Once Again, We'll Fly!

I'll Love You Anyway

Worship Dances on the Dew

Only Believe

He Lights My Way

Angelic Warriors

Sweet Anointing

The Cross of Calvary's Hill

Did You Ever Feel?

Just Around the Bend

Gatekeeper in God's Kingdom

He'll Give Joy in the Journey

Love's Kaleidoscope Displayed

Look Up for Your Redemption Draws Near

Abiding in God's Presence

The Boundary of Heaven Extended

Warriors for Jesus

Resting in His Shadow

Wait upon the Vision

Sword of the Spirit

Winds of Change

Life-giving Words

I Walk in the Midst of My Children

Lift the Load

Healer of My Soul and Mender of My Heart

Solace in the Lord

My Heart Will Sing Your Praise

To Dwell in His Shadow

Fragrance of Springtime

I Will Walk a Faith Walk

What Causes God's Son to Shine

NOVEMBER 1

I'll Love You Anyway

Lord, it really doesn't matter if I stand in silent pain;
Or if I cannot smell the fragrance inside torrential rains,
And it doesn't really matter if the thunder clouds are low;
If they hover like a shadow and follow everywhere I go.
For, you see, I've made a vow to love You anyway,
To know that You are with me, when I am feeling most afraid.
I understand that trials give me strength inside the storm;
Even when my earthly body feels so weary, tired and worn.
So, no matter WHAT the circumstance, I will Love You Anyway;
Whether in the light of sunshine or in a valley filled with pain.
I will keep my eyes upon You in the midst of where I am;
Knowing NOTHING is impossible when it's left inside YOUR
    plan.
Yes, my heart has made a promise—to Love You Anyway
No matter what the circumstance, I face from day to day!

NOVEMBER 2

WORSHIP DANCES ON THE DEW

Mountain peaks are covered
By clouds of blankets from the night;
Green meadows roll with beauty
As dark skies give way to light.
Again, a new day's dawning
In the presence of the Lord;
As night breaks into morning
And the joy of God flows forth.
Each day He bows from heaven
And leaves His kiss of morning dew;
To cover, refresh, replenish—
Releasing life, once more, anew!
God has the dawn of EVERY day
Safely within His hands;
He pulls back the mist of morning
And blows His breath upon the land.
All creation bows before Him
At the light of each new day;
Giving honor in His presence—
Breaking forth in lovely Praise.
Like the sparkle in a diamond
Worship Dances on the Dew;
Unveiling heaven's promise
Of daily mercies—fresh and new!

ONLY BELIEVE

Faith IS—Oh, So Simple—
Two words—ONLY BELIEVE;
It's putting trust in God alone,
No matter, WHAT, I see!
It's hearing His soft whisper,
In the midst of rushing waves;
It's joining heaven's chorus,
Inside Creation's Praise!
It's pressing in, to Jesus,
With faith to rise above;
It's trusting in His promises,
When I FEEL like giving up!
It's moving in His Spirit,
Where His beauty NEVER fades;
It's walking in His presence;
And standing in His Grace.
Yes, Faith IS—Oh, So Simple—
Two words—ONLY BELIEVE;
It's putting trust in God alone,
No matter, WHAT, I see!

NOVEMBER 4

HE LIGHTS MY WAY

He has set me on this path I walk
He teaches me HIS ways;
He gives me hope when I have none
And grace for stormy days.
He has forgiven when I've failed Him
And showers me with love;
He bestows His tender kindness
And pours His mercy from above.
He's always there to lead me
Even when I try and run away;
I find that He's forever faithful
And I cannot help but stand amazed.
He guides me on a fragrant path
By His Spirit and His Truth;
He shines His Word within me
And makes the crooked, straight and smooth.
I don't have to grope in darkness
When I walk within His love;
Nor do I have to strive to overcome
So that I can rise above.
I only need to know Him
As my Savior and My friend;
To trust Him with my heart and soul
And all I have within.
For He is there to light my way
As He guides me down this road;
It was He who set me on THIS path
And it will be HE who leads me home.

ANGELIC WARRIORS

As You gaze across creation and ALL that You have made;
May the door to Your ear open, as You hear the prayers I pray.
May You send Angelic Warriors throughout the atmosphere;
Give them breakthrough for arrival, and HELP them, to get here!
For, I, cry unto You, Lord, and believe that You will move;
That heaven's door WILL open, even when, ALL hell, breaks
     loose.
When the battle is so fierce and I feel I can't go on;
Will You send Angelic Warriors and cause this warfare to be won!
Invade consuming darkness, until it rolls up like a scroll;
As Your mighty forces enter and take position for control.
Like Daniel, I, stand waiting, for YOUR answers to come through;
I have sent my prayers to heaven—and NOW, I put my trust in
     YOU!
So, hear this servant's heart and this cry of desperate need;
Send Your Angels, Lord, from Heaven—to Come and Fight for
     Me!

NOVEMBER 6

SWEET ANOINTING

I know not where the wind comes from,
Yet, I do not doubt it's there;
I cannot SEE it, with my eyes,
BUT—I can FEEL it in the air.
God's Spirit moves in much the same—
I cannot see Him with my eyes;
But I can smell His lovely fragrance
And His Power—recognize!
Sometimes He blows His breath
Upon my heart in such a way;
That He calms my fiercest storms
And speaks, PEACE, to crashing waves.
He comforts me in sorrow
When I feel I can't go on;
He carries me in trials
When I'm weary, tired and worn.
His wisdom is my mantle
His counsel leads me through;
He merely SPEAKS to mountains
And they are forced to move!
But most of all, He points me
To the foot of heaven's throne;
Where angels cry out, "Holy"
And streets are paved with gold.
It's there I'm in God's presence
And yielded to HIS Will;
Lost in Sweet Anointing
And Holy Spirit Filled.
I am captured for the Kingdom
By God's mercy and His grace;
He gives me every THING I need
To run a most successful race.

So, even though I cannot see Him
I have no doubt that He is there;
For, He's the breath upon the wind—
And He's the fragrance in the air.

NOVEMBER 7

THE CROSS OF CALVARY'S HILL

It's the scars that will remind us
Of God's redeeming grace;
It's His precious love that binds us,
To His gentle warm embrace.
For God's Spirit comes in comfort,
To restore sweet peace within;
The Master's touch is always faithful;
To heal and make us whole again.
He, too, has scars and memories
That remind of bitter pain;
But the price He paid on Calvary,
Wipes away each ugly stain.
The scars are just reminders
That victory comes through loss;
When we turn our eyes to Jesus,
And see His LOVE upon a Cross.
For His love sets grace in motion,
With redemptive power to heal;
When we lay our burdens down—
At the Cross of Calvary's Hill!

November 8

Did You Ever Feel?

Did you ever feel the presence of the Lord in such a way;
That no matter WHAT the circumstance, you had peace to guide
your way?
Did you ever feel that in the end, everything would work out fine;
Even though the final outcome didn't look good at the time?
Did you ever feel a peace within, just knowing God is by your
side;
In a place of peaceful refuge, where you could run and hide?
Did you ever feel that hard times, weren't really meant to bring
you harm;
Instead, just draw you closer to the Father's loving arms?
Did you ever feel that God was near, in the middle of the trial;
When you felt you couldn't make it or go another mile?
Well, sometimes, our understanding, must go PAST what eyes
reveal;
To the depth within our hearts, where we KNOW that God is
REAL!
So, even in the bad times when we've been shaken to the core;
By faith, may we keep going, with our eyes upon the Lord!

NOVEMBER 9

JUST AROUND THE BEND

I looked around the corner, and was so surprised to see;
The long awaited blessings, just staring back at me!
Sometimes I got discouraged and stumbled in my faith;
I couldn't see the finish line, nor the ending of the race.
But, I held on through every trial and continued to believe;
For, I knew to NOT give up—for one day I would SEE!
And sure enough, Around the Bend, I saw the tunnel's light;
And I knew, inside this weary soul, the end was now in sight!
Fatigue would never keep me from the blessings I could see;
So, I endured and kept on going , in this race marked out for me!
Sorrow turned to joy and laughter turned to praise;
As I headed for the finish line, and the ending of the race!
Finally, in the distance, I could see the streets of gold;
And I knew there was no blessing, that my Father would
    withhold!
For, EVERYTHING He promised, was right there in front of ME;
Heaven's Door Became the Entrance, and His Love Became the
    Key!

Gatekeeper in God's Kingdom

Lord, I'd rather be a gatekeeper within Your palace walls;
Than to dwell among the wicked who have no love of God.
Yes, I'd rather be a servant in what You've called me, Lord, to do;
Standing safe within Your presence and always seeking more of
    You!
Yielded ALWAYS to Your Spirit—transformed, healed and
    renewed;
Cloaked in robes of righteousness and living daily in Your truth.
Lord, I'd love to be Your servant held close in Your embrace;
Just soaking in Your presence and leaning on Your Grace.
Yes, Lord, I'd rather be a gatekeeper within Your palace walls;
Than to dwell among the wicked in a world where there's no God!

NOVEMBER 11

HE'LL GIVE JOY IN THE JOURNEY

Life's unexpected detours so often cause our faith to grow;
When we have to trust the Lord, to show the way to go.
But we will NEVER walk alone, when our eyes are placed on Him;
He will lead us safely through, and give us inner peace within.
He will open brand-new doors, and cover us with love;
We can count upon His promise, to guide us from above.
He has seen His plan for us, and knows the road that we must
    take;
But He'll stay right by our side, He won't abandon or forsake!
As we step out and follow Jesus, there's no need to be afraid;
As we give our ALL to Him, we'll trust that He will lead our way.
His plan is NOW unfolding, and by faith we must walk through;
But He'll Give Us Joy in the Journey, that He's called us to pursue!

LOVE'S KALEIDOSCOPE DISPLAYED

When I think about the Universe and ALL that You have made;
I cannot help but stand in awe, and TRULY be amazed!
For, You, SPOKE upon creation, and caused everything to form;
The light burst through the darkness, and the galaxies were born.
The heaven's took on splendor, across the vast array;
And the brilliance of the stars, became Your Masterpiece
  Displayed.
And then, as if, it weren't enough, You took the time for man;
You breathed, Your breath, within him and formed him with Your
  hand.
You said that it's not good, for him to be alone;
So, You gave to him, a woman—a rare beauty to behold!
Then You dared to ask for fellowship, as Your Spirit bids us,
  "Come"
And You provided us a way to You, through the life of Your own
  Son!
Father, You have thought of everything, to make our lives
  complete;
You've given us, Your beauty, and placed within us, STRENGTH!
You've splashed exquisite colors, across the open sky;
And created Love's Sweet Promise, that, FOREVER, will abide.
Yes, You, created ALL that IS—You put the Universe in place;
And then, You, opened a star-filled portal, at the foot of heaven's
  gate.
Even, NOW, You're ever watching, through Love's Kaleidoscope
  Displayed,
The Beauty of Your Splendor—and ALL That You Have Made!

NOVEMBER 13

LOOK UP FOR YOUR REDEMPTION DRAWS NEAR

(Read Luke 21:7–28)

I looked inside God's Word today, and was chilled down to the
bone;
For I realized just how close we are, before we meet Him at His
Throne!
There's never been in history, a time in which we live;
Where the scriptures have unfolded and lined up from end to
end.
You see, many things are happening within the Spirit realm;
And if you don't believe it, go and read it for yourself!
God has told us what to watch for, exactly where to set our eyes;
Because He doesn't want us panicked or taken by surprise.
He's given us a blueprint of all we must watch for;
So we wouldn't be in fear as we wait upon the Lord.
He said be not misled by the deception you will hear;
For some will say they're God and claim the end is near.
But do not be persuaded to believe them in their lies
For there's only ONE Messiah and His name is Jesus Christ.
Next you'll hear of widespread wars AND rumors that prevail;
There will be turmoil in the nations and many kingdom's fall and
fail.
Earthquakes and famines and sickness will blanket the earth in a
shroud;
Terror will strike in the heavens and cover the earth with a cloud.
Strange things will begin to happen in the sun, moon and stars
and the skies;
The seas will begin to roar, releasing the wrath of great tides!
Men will be persecuted because of their unfailing faith;
Their souls will be won for the Kingdom, in the midst of a spirit
of hate.

But, my friend, when you see Jerusalem, surrounded on EVERY
  side
By armies from EVERY nation—You'll KNOW where we stand in
  time!
The courage of many will falter as fear comes to swallow the
  earth;
But it's THEN that the heavens will open and the eyes of the
  nations look UP!
Then all of the people shall witness the Messiah in Glory and
  Truth
Every lie will be instantly broken and every veil be completely
  removed.
At that moment the King of the Ages, adorned by the Father
  above;
Will come to redeem His creation and restore all that was given
  up.
So, remember, my friend, His IS Coming, it won't be long 'til He's
  here
For He says when these things are ALL happening—
LOOK UP—FOR YOUR REDEMPTION DRAWS NEAR!

ABIDING IN GOD'S PRESENCE

Abiding in God's Presence
Is where my heart does long to dwell;
Far from outside influence
In that supernatural realm.
Just breathing in His Glory
With every breath I take;
Captured in His presence
In a place completely safe.
Lost within His shadow
Covered beneath His veil;
In the anointing of His presence—
That's where I truly long to dwell.
There is NO place any greater
My soul would ever want to be;
Than in the presence of my Jesus
And His ALL-consuming love for me!

NOVEMBER 15

THE BOUNDARY OF HEAVEN EXTENDED

To walk in the presence of Jesus
And drink from the Spirit's own hand;
Is a treasure of unending value
That most cannot understand.
For it's the Boundary of Heaven Extended
It's the love of the Father to man;
It's the hope of our blessed redeemer
In His overall masterful plan.
It's the gift that was so freely given
In order that all could come in;
It's a privilege and honor of knowing
Jesus, as savior and friend.

NOVEMBER 16

WARRIORS FOR JESUS

The heavens roll back, the sky opens wide;
Praises go forth and set demons to flight.
The angels disperse to wage war even NOW;
Fighting strongholds of darkness that cover like clouds.
The battle is God's and the victory complete;
Through the worshiper's song and the saint's dancing feet.
There is power in praise when a heart lifts to sing;
There is strength for today to set each captive free.
Marching on with great shouts, we as warriors demand;
Defeat to the darkness and light in the land.
Anointed in strength, we claim victory in praise;
We are Warriors for Jesus, standing firm in our faith.

Resting in His Shadow

I'm just resting in the shadow of the Father's Loving Arms;
For, I know that in His presence, He will keep me safe from harm!
I've a peace that comes from standing, beneath the shadow of His
   wings
With a blessing that's unending, and the hope His Spirit brings!
Yes, I'm Resting in His Shadow, and breathing life in Him;
Washed by Heaven's Glory, cleansed and whole within.
Safe from all around me, completely filled with PEACE—
Resting in His Shadow and bowing at His feet!

NOVEMBER 18

WAIT UPON THE VISION

God sows me in His whirlwind—
I cannot pick my landing spot;
For, if my Father is not in it
I am just an empty pod.
BUT, if it's, HE, who truly sows me
Into a rich and fertile ground;
My fruit will be in excess
And my soul be upward bound.
You see, it's only in HIS vision
That my heart will truly know;
All that HE'S prepared
And the mysteries He'll unfold.
So, though the vision seems to tarry
May I put my trust in Him;
Ever hoping in the promise
That's He's given me within.
May I have the faith implanted
To look PAST the things I SEE;
And Wait upon the Vision
That God has placed inside of me.

For the vision is yet for an appointed time; But at the
end it will speak and it will not lie. Though it tarries,
wait for it; Because it will surely come, It will not tarry.

—HABAKKUK 2:3

November 19

Sword of the Spirit

Lord, Your Word is my weapon of warfare,
its power can't be denied;
It's a two-edged Sword of the Spirit—
my constant companion and guide.
It comforts my heart when it's broken,
it binds up the wounds of my soul;
Your Word is like sweet balm from heaven,
that heals and restores and makes whole.
Yes, Your Word, gives strength to my being,
it's life in abundance to me;
Like a light on a hill that's left shining,
for all of the world to see.
It leads me and gives me direction,
it calms the waves in the storm;
Its peace has anointing and power,
to speak to the tempest roar.
Yes, Lord, Your Word is my weapon of warfare,
over time it's been tested and tried;
It's a two-edged Sword of the Spirit—
my constant companion and guide!

WINDS OF CHANGE

Today, I am trusting in Jesus, as we walk side by side, hand in
　　hand;
He has opened the windows of heaven and is fulfilling HIS
　　purpose and plan.
He's positioned my life in His Kingdom, to be strong in the things
　　of God;
He has given me strength for the battle, and prepared me for
　　things I know not.
Yes, my vision has been expanded, to see HIS light on the hill;
I'm expecting great things in the Spirit, from the mysteries He's
　　already revealed.
He has tested and stretched beyond limits, every fiber of my very
　　soul;
He has purified me in His fire, and has brought me forth as fine
　　gold.
Now, I am sensing His season of harvest, for my passion has
　　grown through the pain;
Yes, TODAY, is a new day in Jesus—and I'm sensing HIS Winds
　　of Change!

LIFE-GIVING WORDS

"Power of the Tongue" (Read Proverbs 18:21)

May spoken words from my mouth
Bring forth BLESSING, Lord, today;
Releasing LIFE and never death
In everything that I will say.
I know great power does reside
Within my EVERY word;
They can damage or bring healing—
They can soothe or cause deep hurt!
May I speak positive confessions
That bring forth the signs of life;
Not hateful chilling words
That cause death's wretched head to rise.
Today may my TRUE heart be seen
By every single word I speak;
For, like a mirror, they reflect—
All that's inside me!
So may the words that flow from me
Refrain from ALL that's not of You;
Instead, I pray You'll touch my heart,
Clean it up and make it new.
May my tongue be never used
To speak a judgment or a curse;
Instead, Lord, give me POWER
For ONLY—Life-giving Words!

I WALK IN THE MIDST OF MY CHILDREN

As I Walk in the Midst of My Children, My ears are alert to each
  cry;
I see and I hear every heartbeat—NOTHING escapes My eye!
The blessings I've promised are coming, believe that I do ALL
  things;
Trust in Me for each answer, and the healing My Spirit brings.
When My children bow in My presence, My heart is stirred to
  move;
And I promise to show you exactly, what it is that you are to do.
I meet you each individually, so be prepared and you will know;
That I hear the cries of my people—and I see every heart that's
  bowed low!
So, as I Walk in the Midst of My Children, I promise to be there
  for you;
I'll answer the cries of EACH heart, for there is NOTHING that I
  cannot do!

LIFT THE LOAD

Only You can give me hope, Lord; my answers lie in YOU;
I know that You will lead me, and help me make it through!
This crooked path before me, becomes straight before my eyes;
As You turn my darkest hour, into my brightest light!
For the hope within my heart, rests in YOU, alone;
Only You can raise me up—and only You, can Lift the Load!

NOVEMBER 24

HEALER OF MY SOUL AND MENDER OF MY HEART

Sometimes in my journey, I've found that life just seems unfair
And there's often no escaping the heartaches I must bear.
Because circumstances come along and without notice hell
    breaks loose;
And my pathway takes a detour that I didn't want OR choose.
But I find that in the process, if I will keep my eyes on God
He will lead me through the fire—He will guide me in my walk.
His promises are endless and in Him I am secure;
He will not leave me nor forsake me—instead He helps me to
    endure.
He becomes a treasured refuge that my brokenness does seek;
He draws me to His bosom, where He heals my pain and grief.
It's when I keep my eyes on Him, that peace does flood my soul;
Like a spotlight beamed from heaven that restores and makes me
    whole.
You see, it's only in the process that my heart will truly know—
His plan of new beginnings and the blessings He'll unfold.
I know that Jesus puts back pieces that once were torn apart—
For He's the Healer of My Soul and He's the Mender of My Heart!

November 25

Solace in the Lord

God's love soars above the shoreline, of what our earthly eyes
    behold;
And it reaches past the depths, of every single soul.
It pierces through the heavens and the stars that hang in space;
Yet, it easily finds its way, to those who long to see His Face!
You see, there is nowhere on earth, or heavens far above;
That God's Creation will be lost, or found outside His Love.
For, His Love is everlasting, like a circle without end;
It covers heights and depths, and everything therein.
Yes, His Love is all sufficient, and will last forevermore;
And happy is the man, that finds his Solace in the Lord!

MY HEART WILL SING
YOUR PRAISE

Before I was created, You knew exactly who I'd be;
Because, You, Lord, were the potter that precisely fashioned me.
Since then, You've never left me nor ever let me down;
You've always calmed the waves, and kept me from the fear, I'd
    drown.
Yes, You've called me unto You—because THAT'S where I
    belong;
You've instilled within me, HOPE, and given strength to make me
    strong.
You have justified me daily and erased all that I have done;
And though there's evidence against me—I'm STILL covered in
    Your Blood!
Your FAVOR has become, the robe around my soul;
And Your Glory is the beacon, of ALL, my heart does hold!
So, even though I stumble and sometimes fall along the way;
My life will keep its focus and My Heart Will Sing Your Praise!

To Dwell in His Shadow

To dwell in the safety of that secret place;
To abide in the shelter of His Loving Grace!
To be hidden away, by covering wings;
Far from troubles and worries, and everyday things!
To find rest in my soul, and peace deep within;
To be close to His heart, and far from earth's sin.
To Dwell in the Shadow, of the ONE Most High;
Is the most perfect place, I could EVER abide!

NOVEMBER 28

FRAGRANCE OF SPRINGTIME

In the midst of every heartache, and trial along the way;
When I felt as if I'd crumble, and had no strength to even pray,
When the days just seemed so long, and the nights seemed NOT
   to end;
When hope just seemed to vanish, and there was emptiness
   within!
When life seemed overwhelming and I thought my heart would
   stop;
When I screamed and yelled in anger—and my tears gave way to
   sobs,
It was THEN, You sent Your angels, and gave compassion from
   Your throne;
You boosted me with energy, that I KNEW was NOT my own!
You lifted me from bended knees, and dried the tears upon my
   face;
You gave me peace within my heart, and strength for one more
   day.
You led me when I stumbled, and guided with Your hand;
You protected and directed, when I failed to understand!
The storm clouds that surrounded me, are being blown away,
And, NOW, I smell the Springtime—and the freshness of the day!

I Will Walk a Faith Walk

I will NOT draw back
Nor let fear rule within;
I will walk toward Jesus—
And keep my eyes upon HIM!
I know God's MORE than faithful—
His EVERY promise is sure;
My faith will NOT waver—
For I was made to endure.
So even though struggles
May STILL come my way;
I am destined through Jesus
To overcome day by day.
And when I walk with the Lord
I will ALWAYS come through;
I will NOT loose my confidence
But—HIS WILL—pursue!
For I am living my life
In the favor of God;
So I will focus on HIM—
And I Will Walk a Faith Walk!

NOVEMBER 30

WHAT CAUSES GOD'S SON TO SHINE

What does it take in my daily life, to allow the Son to shine—
It takes the power of sowing and reaping, and claiming each
   promise that's mine.
It's the love and the joy of sharing, it's giving in ways that exceed;
It's trusting in Jesus by faith, and believing He'll bring the
   increase.
It's a heart of love for my brother, it's listening with ears to hear;
It's facing each day with God's blessing, and knowing the harvest
   is near.
It's allowing Christ love to overcome, past the problems that arise
   everyday;
It's recognizing God's Holy Spirit, is at work to show me the way.
It's the heart of my loving Father, and His every thought toward
   me;
That causes His Son to freely shine, and His Spirit to set me free.

His Sabbath Rest
Let Not Your Heart Be Troubled
More Than a Conqueror
Waiting Out the Storm
He's Always There
His Strength Will Carry You
Glory Road to Heaven
My Heart Belongs to Him Alone
Abide in the Vine
One Heart
God's Gift of Grace
Burden to Bear
Light at the End of the Tunnel
Walking in His Light
Joy's Promise
The Hope of Victory
Your Plans Concerning Me
Storms of Life
It's Through His Eyes I See
His Love Extended
Light of Your Glory
The Renewing of My Mind
Painted Crimson in the Snow
Love's Eternal Gift
The Most Precious Gift of All
Grace for Today
Quiet Heart
Unveil My Heart to See Your Glory
We Need a Miracle
Roots of Life
It's Beginning to Rain

DECEMBER

DECEMBER 1

HIS SABBATH REST

The weight of my burden, seems so heavy to bear;
And my heart often struggles with overwhelming despair;
But, because I have favor, in the eyes of the Lord;
I can TRUST that He's with me, to carry me forth!
You see, my bondage is broken, when my heart's circumcised;
When I'm yielded COMPLETELY, and to HIM, I am tied.
Yes, HE, gives me rest—He restores and renews;
When my soil remains fertile, and my worries stay few.
It's only in Him, that my TRUE heart is seen;
Do, I trust He is there—do I TRULY believe?
HIS 'Tent of Meeting'—HIS Sabbath Rest,
Draws me to Him, in the midst of my test!
For, my God wants me strong, healthy and whole;
Equipped for the race, and enabled to grow.
He has opened my heart and He's helped me to see;
All of the goodness, that He has for me.
Yes, only HE can give rest, in the midst of my pain;
When I fall on my knees and call out His name.
So, may HIS Glory, come through, every trial and test,
As I walk in HIS peace—into, HIS Sabbath Rest!

Let Not Your Heart Be Troubled

Fear and worry only hinder
The awesome work of God;
They're the opposite of faith
In the midst of where you walk.
So, if you bow your heart in prayer
Be not troubled or afraid;
For, if you KNOW you're going to worry
Then you might as well not pray.
You see, God will only work with
What you CHOOSE to give to Him;
You can either offer faith
OR fear and worry held within.
So, trust Him in your trial
And let His loving peace take hold;
Yes, He'll calm your every fear
If you'll just learn, to let it go.
So, let worry never hinder
All the plans God has for you;
Merely trust Him in the trial
And know that HE will see you through.

MORE THAN A CONQUEROR

If my God is for me
Who dares come against;
Whom should I fear
When He's my defense?
You see, I'm called of God
To conquer this war;
I will NOT lose heart—
I will TRUST in the Lord.
I will NOT be distressed
Nor discontent in this walk;
For I have power and might
In the eyes of my God.
My heart won't give up
Nor will I draw back;
Instead I'll press on
When I am under attack.
I will NOT allow fear
To take hold of my life;
For I am More Than a Conqueror
Through the Lord Jesus Christ!

DECEMBER 4

WAITING OUT THE STORM

I'm so easily tossed by the waves on the sea;
Seems at times the attacks come and overwhelm me.
But the truth DOES remain, down deep in my soul;
That my God is ALIVE, and He is STILL in control.
So, no matter what obstacles, are thrust in my way;
I will stand in HIS strength, having roots that won't sway.
For I KNOW that the answers will come if I stand;
Even when my heart fails and I can't see God's plan.
For the Lord, in His timing, will come rescue and save;
He will deliver me safely, from the winds and the rain.
In those times when I'm desperate, I will trust in the Lord;
I'll cling tightly to Jesus and Just Wait out the Storm.
And when it's all over, I'll be able to see;
That in the worst of it all—He held tightly to me!

DECEMBER 5
HE'S ALWAYS THERE

When all else fails, you will see;
Jesus is there, to care for your needs.
He won't ever leave, or run away;
He'll ALWAYS be there, from day to day!
He's consistent and faithful, He's a loyal friend;
And He's already walked, where you have been.
He's listens to you and your deepest care;
And He lifts you to heights, on the wings of a prayer.

HIS STRENGTH WILL CARRY YOU

It's the place where your heart's broken
That HIS strength just filters through;
For it's when you feel your weakest,
God's there, uplifting you!
It's the times you hurt the worst
When your faith just seems to grow;
It's only THEN, you learn to trust,
And let your burdens go.
It's the heartache and the pain
That will bring you to your knees;
It's finding joy in the journey,
In spite of what you feel or see.
It's knowing Jesus never leaves you,
Within the fire's scorching heat;
Instead, He's there to shield you,
Until His purpose is complete.
So, when your world begins to crumble,
And your heart just breaks in two;
Embrace His precious grace,
And HIS Strength Will Carry You!

GLORY ROAD TO HEAVEN

I know not what tomorrow brings, but I KNOW, God has a plan;
And even in, life's unsure things, I must learn to take a stand.
For my feet are firmly planted upon the sturdy rock;
And my heart will never waiver, when it comes to trusting God.
The winds may howl and oceans rise, and tempest storms may
    come;
But I've set my eyes upon the Cross, and put my faith upon God's
    Son.
For, you see, I'm just a pilgrim, on a pathway headed home;
I was never made to wander, nor just set my sights to roam.
Instead, my heart is focused upon the journey's end;
Where earthly things will pass away—and NEW life will begin!
So, today I'll keep my heart in tune with where His Spirit leads;
And I'll run the race marked out for me, no matter WHAT I see.
For when my life is over and it's all been said and done;
My destiny will be in HIM, as one who chose, to overcome!

DECEMBER 8

MY HEART BELONGS
TO HIM ALONE

My head lies upon my Father's breast
I hear the rhythm His heart makes;
I am drawn to His own bosom—
In His presence, my heart quakes!
He has stirred me by His Spirit
To a closer place in Him;
He has captured me forever
And cleansed my hardened heart of sin.
My discernment increases daily
As I listen to His Word;
My ears are tuned to truth
And my sight's no longer blurred.
For NOW, I know His voice
No more counterfeit for me;
I have tasted of His goodness
And His Grace has set me free.
I won't be drawn off course again
Nor impassioned by worldly things;
For my future NOW has vision—
My eyes are set upon the King.
Yes, I lay my head upon His breast
I feel His breath upon my soul;
I am empowered for His Kingdom—
My Heart Belongs to Him Alone!

DECEMBER 9

ABIDE IN THE VINE

(Read John 15:1–8)

Abide in the Vine, through calm and through storms;
Stay attached to the branch, the ONLY true source!
Yes, He's the TRUE VINE, and the gardener of ALL;
He cuts and He prunes, making fruitful and strong.
So, always take care to live in the Vine;
Daily, growing in strength—and light from the "SON" shine.
For a branch CAN'T produce, luscious fruit day to day;
If it's not attached to the vine, and severed away!
But IF, in the Vine, you are pruned by His hands;
You can ask what you will, and then trust in His Plans!
For each TRUE disciple, will ALWAYS produce;
A bountiful harvest and ripe luscious fruit!

DECEMBER 10

ONE HEART

Lord, I have heard Your voice, in the midst of deepest grief;
I have felt Your loving arms, and I have heard Your Spirit speak.
It's when I crawl into Your lap and lay my head upon Your breast;
That You soothe my ravage soul, and breathe Your breath into
   MY chest!
Lord, You've called me to come higher and set my self apart;
You've bridged the gap between us, with revelation to my heart.
Surely, I can truly say, I'm in Your presence, Lord;
Whether on the mountaintop, or the ocean's deepest floor.
For, You've spoken depths of mystery, for that which is to come;
And You've given me the blueprints of the race that I'm to run.
I'm blessed with GREATER vision, to overcome and rise above;
As You teach me, Lord, to FLY—Upon Your Wings of Love!
So, I will take the time, to FULLY enter into REST;
I will crawl into YOUR lap, and lay my head upon YOUR breast.
For, it's in that place of solitude, that I'll have ears to hear;
Your Promises of Victory, sweetly whispered in my ear!
Yes, I will come up higher and set myself apart;
In that place of Heaven's Glory—Where there ONLY beats,
ONE HEART!

DECEMBER 11

GOD'S GIFT OF GRACE

Lord, I pray that my life
In response to Your Grace;
Would be righteous and pure
As I seek Your sweet face.
May the fruit of Your love
Burn with passion inside;
May I humbly be used
As a vessel of Christ.
For Your salvation's a gift
It will NEVER be earned;
It is only by Grace
That my hard heart can turn.
So, I pray that the Grace
You so graciously give;
Won't be fruitless and void
Through the lifestyle I live.
I pray that my heart
Will ALWAYS seek and pursue;
A life that is righteous—
And gives honor to You!

DECEMBER 12

BURDEN TO BEAR

God would not give me
A burden to bear;
To only cause grief
And overwhelming despair.
Along with each burden
He'll give me faith to believe;
He'll give me hope in the midst
Of all I Hear, Feel, and See!

DECEMBER 13

LIGHT AT THE END OF THE TUNNEL

There's a Light at the End of the Tunnel,
That gives the direction I need;
To shine in the places of darkness,
And illuminate God's path for me!
For His light overwhelms ANY darkness,
There's NO place, at all, it can hide;
It yields to God's Glory and Power—
It's instantly GONE, in the Light!
So, I'll keep my eyes on the "Son" shine,
And walk in it's bright, intense ray;
I'll follow the leading of Jesus,
Knowing HIS light will guide me today!
Yes, There's a Light at the End of the Tunnel,
That gives the direction I need;
To shine in the places of darkness,
And illuminate God's path for me!

December 14

Walking in His Light

Once we were in darkness
But NOW, we walk in LIGHT;
We've the nature of rebirth
For we are NOW alive in Christ.
You see, Light is IN the Life
Of Jesus Christ, Himself;
In the LIGHT there is no darkness
There's no place for it to dwell.
He's the fullness of the Glory—
He's the Message sent from God;
He came to set men free;
By HIM, we've been blood bought!
For in Jesus there is NO darkness—
The Light in Him is LIFE;
Through Him the Glory of His Father,
Cannot help but brightly shine.
Now Christians all around the world
Share the Light of Christ within;
Their very lives are joined together
Because their hearts are turned to Him!
The Holiness that we now walk in
Has become that which gives us life;
For the LIGHT that burns within us
Most surely IS the Life of Christ!

DECEMBER 15

JOY'S PROMISE

Persistence in prayer, in the midst of it all;
Through the darkness of night—into the presence of God.
Ever faithful is He, when my cries touch His ear;
When I press through the pain, and to Him I draw near.
Understanding that PRAISE, is my weapon to use;
When my heart has been wounded, overwhelmed, and abused.
Finding my warfare, becomes strong when I praise;
For my worship is worthy, in HIS Holy Place.
His presence is drawn to the depths of my soul;
When I run from my SELF and I head to HIS throne.
So, I'll stand in my nighttime and know who HE is;
I will take every problem, and I'll make them HIS!
You see, He's aware of the trials and the struggles I face
But His promise is sure—He'll NOT leave nor forsake!
Because, MY God is triumphant, even when I can't see;
And His answers WILL come—in the midst of my need!

The Hope of Victory

God's recipes for miracles so often come within the flames;
Where my walk is called "salvation" and my gates are renamed
"praise."
You see, it's IN the midst of troubles, I will witness His strong
hand;
When the fire FEELS the hottest and escape's NOT in the plan.
It's only God's deliverance that can truly keep me safe;
Inside the fiery furnace and its overwhelming flames.
In this place He guards my heart and breathes peace within my
soul;
He refines me in the process and brings me forth as purest gold.
My life becomes a witness for all the world to see
The power of deliverance and the Hope of Victory!

YOUR PLANS CONCERNING ME

I've never reached a depth so low that Your love could not break
  through;
Nor have I strayed so far away as to separate from You.
For even at the valley's floor, Your hand could still reach me;
To stir the hope within my heart and set this captive free.
Lord, even in life's deepest pit, it was Your unfailing love;
That intervened from heaven's throne, to reach down and pick
  me up!
You brandished spear and javelin against my darkest foe;
You contended with my enemy and released his harsh control.
You disgraced and put to shame those who sought my life;
And all the while You loved me and never once removed Your
  eyes.
You chased away my enemies like chaff before the wind;
And drove them to a path, dark and slippery for them.
But all the while, You led my way, and kept MY footsteps firm;
You taught me on my journey, and many lessons I did learn.
And though I often stumbled, I never truly fell;
Instead, You always lifted me, up to a higher realm.
So, as I travel down life's road, my heart will always be;
Set upon YOUR Will, oh Lord, and Your Plans Concerning Me!

DECEMBER 18
STORMS OF LIFE

Lord, sometimes all I see are storms
And the power of their strength;
I find myself in darkness
And I feel as if I'll sink.
I dash about here and there
Desperate to prepare;
I seek to find the answers
EVERY place and EVERYwhere!
Seems I feel an obligation
To ALWAYS know the plan;
When I think I'M in control
I feel I THEN can understand.
But what I fail to see
Is I cannot stop the wind;
I cannot fight the battles
That roar and rage within.
So I often find I'm focused
On the pit of deep despair;
Instead of seeking truth
From the one who's most aware.
So I ask for help, Lord Jesus
When I stand amidst the storm;
I look to YOU for answers
When I'm tattered, tired, and worn.
Pierce my soul and help me see
That there really IS a plan;
Even when I'm tossed about
And cannot seem to understand.
May Your Spirit blow away the dross
And cause MY will to bend;
Please help me make it through the storm
And build YOUR character within.

IT'S THROUGH HIS EYES I SEE

If my vision gets distorted, it will surely shut me down;
Because, how I see MYSELF determines WHERE I will be found.
I want to bathe in HIS anointing, knowing who I truly am;
Prepared for EVERY battle, secure within God's Plan!
I am more than just a conqueror—I am the head, I'm not the tail;
And because my life belongs to Christ, I know I CAN prevail.
I cannot have distorted vision, in HIM, I must stay strong;
I must persevere through trials, and always KNOW, whose side,
    I'm on.
You see, everything, I'll ever need—lives deep inside of me;
For God has given me, HIS SPIRIT—and It's Through HIS Eyes, I
    See!

HIS LOVE EXTENDED

Lord, how can I sit at your table
When I harbor unforgiveness within;
How can I partake of Your Glory
When my life is in bondage to sin?
My heart MUST receive Your conviction
To confess that which keeps me from You;
That separates me from Your presence
And the blessings of God I pursue.
For Your love will NEVER abandon
But my heart MUST respond to Your call;
To be free from the darkness that hinders
And cleansed from the things not of God.
So, today, I bow in my weakness
And I ask for YOUR strength in my life;
I humbly confess and repent of each sin
And ALL that has kept me from Christ.
Through Your unfailing love and forgiveness
I will continue my purpose in You;
Keeping my eyes ALWAYS focused
On the things You have called me to do.
May I find myself at Your table
Welcomed to eat of the feast;
Rejoicing with glory and honor and praise
For the love You've extended to me!

LIGHT OF YOUR GLORY

May the Light of Your Glory shine through my life;
As I seek humbly to follow Your way;
Cause the eyes of my heart to focus ONLY on YOU,
Let the light of YOUR love be displayed.
May the truth of Your Word be ALL that will shine—
Like a ray in the midst of a storm;
Giving hope to the hopeless and sight to the blind,
Like a compass to heaven's own door.
Set my life to be in position,
For the light of YOUR love to shine through;
Draw my heart by Your own precious Spirit,
And cause my foundation to be built upon YOU!
Anoint me, Oh Lord, as YOUR lighthouse,
And place me where I can be used;
Let the light of Your Son be a beacon to all
Cause the light of YOUR love to pierce through.
May the Light of Your Glory shine on and on,
As a burst of hope in the night;
Set a course for lost hearts to find Jesus,
As the darkness gives way to the light.
May the light never dull as it ages,
Or grow dim in the midst of life's storms;
Instead cause it's beam to grow brighter,
As the Light of Your Glory pours forth!

THE RENEWING OF MY MIND

God sees me at my worst, and He knows where I have been;
He's aware of all my failures and every single sin.
But my Father has a vision with a future and a plan;
To draw me unto Jesus and make me more like Him.
He reveals to me His Glory and He opens up my eyes;
He changes me from inside out, by the Renewing of My Mind.
So, I will not walk in blindness with a veil upon my eyes;
Instead, I'll see Him clearly, and rise to greater heights.
I'll go BEYOND my comprehension, and let HIM change my life;
I'll walk in Rays of Glory—knowing He is by my side.
He transforms me with precision, He opens eyes that once were
    blind;
He perfects me for His Kingdom, by the Renewing of My Mind.

DECEMBER 23

PAINTED CRIMSON
IN THE SNOW

The air was still, the breeze was crisp
On that chilly winter morn;
My heart had just been pierced
By a hurtful, prickly thorn.
I stood before the windowpane
Seeking solace in the peace;
When I spied a gorgeous cardinal
Nestled safely in a tree.
His little, tiny figure
Was like crimson in the snow;
God had sent a gift from heaven
Touched my heart and gave me HOPE!
You see, ONLY God can understand
The daily perils I go through;
He cares about each heartache
Every tattered place and bruise.
But in the midst of turmoil
I find Him faithful day to day;
To exhibit tiny miracles
That give me hope along the way.
He shows Himself in little things—
And allows me to behold;
The love He holds inside, for ME—
Painted Crimson in the Snow!

LOVE'S ETERNAL GIFT

The Christmas Season is repeated
Year and year again;
So that we'll remember
What You have done for man.
It summons men, to stop and ponder
Who's truly "Center of It All";
As we turn our thoughts to Jesus
And yield our hearts to You, Oh God.
Help us, Lord, to enter in—
Into the presence of the King;
And to the promises of peace
Through all this season brings.
May we NOT be prone to wander
Instead, RECEIVE all that You have done;
May we RETURN to what's been given
Through the life of Your own Son.
May You help us to maintain, Lord
The truth of who YOU are;
Like the wise men in the fields
Faithfully following Your star!
Today, as this world remembers
The Christ Child sent from YOU;
May hearts be changed forever
And lives be made brand new.
May this season bring reflection
Of Love's Eternal Gift—
The Birth of Your Son, Jesus,
Born, That Men May Live!

DECEMBER 25

THE MOST PRECIOUS
GIFT OF ALL

Lord, how can I repay, the price You paid for me;
So many years ago, upon the Cross of Calvary?
You see, I can truly see it, in my mind so very clear;
The steps You took to give ME life, to rip the veil and draw me
    near!
I can hear the conversation between the Father and the Son;
Of all that You'd endure, so that MY heart, could be won.
You left Your Home in Glory, Your Kingdom and Your Throne;
To come into MY world—and give, Your life, to lead ME home.
Just a tiny baby, wrapped in swaddling clothes;
Laying in a manger—the Gift of Life And Hope!
To grow in simple lifestyle, unlike Your Kingly Role;
You gave up heaven's treasures and the comfort of Your Throne!
And THEN, the time DID come, for You to sacrifice it all;
It was the plan for all the ages, it gave redemption for the fall!
Your Blood was shed upon that Cross, as YOU became a lamb;
And all of time stood silent, across the heavens and the land.
It was done, YES, it was finished, and the plan fell into place;
It's where a King became a baby, and then a man who poured out
    GRACE!
From the grave, You rose to life, and returned to Heaven's Throne;
And You did it ALL for ME—You made me, Lord, Your Own.
The gift You gave was priceless, it has made me who I am;
A Child Redeemed by Grace—Forever Grateful, to the Lamb!
And even now, I wait for You, and watch for You to come;
As YOUR plan, comes to fruition, and the FINAL victory's won!

GRACE FOR TODAY

Wherever you are—
Be—ALL—there;
Rest in God's grace
Like the birds of the air.
Take time to listen
To His voice each day;
Do not worry or fret—
Do NOT be afraid.
Be anxious for nothing
Take every care to the Lord;
His peace will enfold—
Your heart, He will guard.
Leave in His hands
Your burdens EACH day;
He will bear them in love—
And give you—Grace for Today!

DECEMBER 27

QUIET HEART

The heart that listens quietly
As the baby sparrow sings;
Will also hear the flutter
In the sound of angels' wings.
They will feel the tender presence
And God's breath upon their soul;
They will see the heart of Jesus
And the beauty He bestows.
The heart that takes the time
To be still and seek God's face;
Will be the heart that truly lives
Within the love of His embrace.

UNVEIL MY HEART TO SEE YOUR GLORY

As I come into Your presence, Lord,
Unveil My Heart that I can see;
The splendor of Your Glory
And Your awesome love for me.
I will praise You from my inner depths—
Where my soul cries out for More;
I will seek You, Lord, in worship
Yes, I will knock on heaven's door!
May You remove all chains that bind,
That hold me captive and afraid;
I pray You'll break them by Your Spirit—
And lead me boldly through Your gates.
Lord, revive my heart in worship
Set my spirit free to Praise;
Remove everything that hinders
And let me SEE You face to face.
May I come into Your presence
And Your beauty, Lord, behold;
Unveil My Heart to See Your Glory—
And the Splendor of Your Throne!

DECEMBER 29

WE NEED A MIRACLE

Lord, We Need a Miracle—there's not a thing MORE, we can do;
Except STAND upon Your promises, and put our trust in YOU!
Every door WE try to open, just closes in our face;
We are more and more discouraged, and slowly losing faith!
Seems the walls are closing in, and there's no hope to face the
    day;
Please help us, Lord, to trust YOU, and take this fear away!
For, we know You won't abandon us, nor leave us on our own;
We've loved You much to long, to think You'd leave us all alone!
Lord, we are totally dependant, upon YOU to lead our way;
We are desperate for Your answers—We Need a Miracle TODAY!

Roots of Life

When the storms of life DO come,
And harsh winds begin to blow;
It's THEN and only THEN—
You know how DEEP your roots DO grow!
For if they're on the surface,
You'll find yourself adrift;
Never truly planted,
Instead, just blowing in the wind!
BUT, if your roots are deep
And watered from above;
You'll have strength for ANY storm,
And every element that comes!

IT'S BEGINNING TO RAIN

We are entering the Realm of His Glory,
Where the abundance is about to release;
A season of great expectation,
And heaven's great rain of increase!
Yes, it's the dawning of a new day,
Discouragement will no longer bring pain;
For God's Spirit is being poured forth
And NOW, It's Beginning to Rain!
The blessings of God are falling
Hearts are touched to receive;
All that the Lord has prepared
To those who will trust and believe.
Promises long gone and forgotten,
Will arise in the air that we breathe;
Fulfillment with great celebration
For all that we're going to see.
There is hope in His Holy Provision—
An anointing, in abundance, THIS year;
For the floodgates of heaven are opening,
And the Glory of God is NOW here!
It's the promise of all we have hoped for,
The answers to every prayer prayed;
This year, a Fulfillment of Blessings
Look Up—It's Beginning to Rain!

TO CONTACT THE AUTHOR

SowinSeed4Jesus@aol.com

www.SowinSeedMinistry.com